Divorce

as 'Required' by

Scripture

(Help for Victims of
Ungodly Marriages)

by R.A. Ross

Divorce as 'Required' by Scripture

(Help for Victims of Ungodly Marriages)

ISBN-13: 978-0-9771517-0-7
ISBN-10: 0-9771517-0-0

Published by
Deeper Doctrine™
P.O. Box 291
Grantham, PA
17027-0291

Printed in the USA by
Morris Publishing
3212 E. Highway 30
Kearney, NE 68847
800-650-7888

Dedication

To my Father in Heaven, whom I have now sought with my whole heart for over half of my six decades—may this book show my Savior & Lord Jesus Christ to be speaking truth when He said:

> John 15:5, "I am the vine; you are the branches. If a man remains in me and I in him, he will bear much fruit; apart from me you can do nothing. (NIV)

To my dear Christian wife of seventeen years, my one-hundred-fold wife—may you increase in Christ, even to a one-thousand-fold wife....

To my church family, where I have pastored (half-time) during the writing of this book—may this book help us reach out to victims of ungodly marriages, to help our small church grow into a full-fledged congregation.

Table of Contents

Part I
Bible Bases

Part II
Applications and Additional Assertions

Introduction

Family ties are one of the most important issues of our time. Such ties are important to any era when people care about God's institution of marriage and family. The primary foundation of any civilized society is the family. Civilized family life needs all of the protections it can get.

Naturally then, when family ties are easily broken without good cause, this God given strength of any nation begins to crumble. Therefore religious and governmental leaders do well to insure that family ties are not broken. However when efforts to hold marriages (and families) together are taken too far, other strengths of family life also begin to crumble.

This book about Bible divorces looks deeply into why God "ties and unties" families, from Genesis to

Revelation.... God's first choice has never been divorce, and the related crumbling of a society. On the other hand, there is another crumbling He does not want. It occurs in the hearts of spouses and children who are badly mistreated. This includes benign neglect, obvious hatred, and physical battering.

Our Father in Heaven is the God who overcomes evil with good--and sometimes He appears to break His own rules in order to do this. Consider the story of Shiphrah and Puah near the beginning of the second book of the Bible.

In Exodus chapter one there came a new king to the Egyptian throne. This king saw that the Israelites were multiplying too fast and that their numbers might threaten his kingdom. He oppressed the Israelites with forced labor but they still multiplied in number. Then this king told the Hebrew midwives Shiphrah and Puah to let baby girls live, but to kill the baby boys at birth. Shiphrah and Puah not only disobeyed the king, but they apparently lied to him (verse 19). Then our Father in Heaven rewarded these two midwives with families of their own. The "good," which God used to overcome this "evil" king, apparently came from lies....

How could God do such a thing? Has He not forbidden lying? Yes, His Commandment number nine opposes lying. God even forbids deceiving of one another (Leviticus 19:11). However our God also allows unusual means, like lying and deceiving, when it will save lives. (See Joshua 2:1-14, I Samuel 19:14, 17, and others.)

Shiphrah & Puah apparently had done just that—they lied (or deceived) to save the lives of innocent baby boys. They also may not have known that God specifically opposed lying. The Ten Commandments were not written until many years after their "situation" with the king had passed.

Let's suppose that Shiphrah & Puah's natural conscience did somewhat bother them. Let's suppose that they even prayed beforehand about what they did. This writer would then believe that they were "blameless before God," in regard to their actions.

This issue of being "blameless before God" is very important to understanding why some marriages need to be "untied." Blamelessness *before God* is more important than blamelessness *before man*. Consider the sailors who threw Jonah overboard. They cried out to the LORD when they thought they were about to commit murder. They begged the LORD not to hold them accountable.... He seems to have "agreed" with their actions by calming the waves. (See Jonah 1:14-15.)

A tougher case to consider is also mentioned right up front in this book. Some Bibles say that a man who "puts away" his wife (without a certificate of divorce) may be at fault for her acts of adultery. The King James Version says, in Matthew 5:32, that such a husband, "...causeth her to commit adultery." Some of these wives would then be "blameless before God," in their apparent acts of adultery. Many other wives would not be blameless—before God or man. This book will get into situations of both kinds.

This does not mean that "situation ethics" should ever be carried beyond Bible models, but it does prove a point about God. He seems to delight in taking care of the underdog, even when it means breaking one of His own rules.

Many a wife has been an "underdog" in her own home, and some husbands too. This book about divorces found in the Bible shows any number of times when God not only *allowed* divorce but actually *"required"* divorce. This author intends to show that one of God's motives in these divorces was to protect underdogs. This protection would especially apply to an abused underdog.

Everyone seems to agree that God is love, (see verse 8 of 1st John 4). God is also wrathful, jealous, long suffering, creative, prophetic, sovereign, etc. Part of His "jealously" includes being protective. One could say that He jealously protects His own creation, and surely we could agree that He protects the institution of family. Disagreement comes when we discuss how He protects family. For example, does the Word of God say that wedding vows are irrevocable—despite many years of physical abuse? Or, have some men made that rule?

Folks who stand by rules are valuable, but when they refuse to look at needful exceptions to the rules, they often create oppression. Their intent may be very good, but the outcome may be very bad. Their rules, like the rules of the Pharisees, do more harm than good. These kind of people, many of whom claim to be dedicated Christians, just cannot seem to see what God sees...in terms of a love that protects. Yes, this kind of love looks at the *rules*--but it also looks at the *results* of applying the rules. (Results here include the underdog spouse and also any children.) When the love-balance gets too far out-of-balance for too long, God is likely to cause or allow some remedy—even if it "breaks the rules."

Suppose that God would allow us to be guests at a board meeting with angels--angels who are helping Pastor Stiffneck change his mind about divorce. These angels have already tried to help Betty Battered but she has not listened to them as much as she has to her pastor and the church board. For almost a decade Betty's church officials have known about her being battered by her husband. On many occasions Betty has begged for help but has basically been told that she married this guy for better or worse—and that the worse will not go on forever. Betty finally drops out of church but will not leave her husband. The angels again tell her to leave but she thinks that she just might save her marriage if she stays. Betty finally has a complete nervous breakdown and ends up on the streets as a "bag lady." One day Pastor Stiffneck sees Betty but cannot believe it is really her. He stops to talk but her eyes fail to recognize him. Just then one angel tells this pastor that Betty's condition is primarily his fault. He weeps almost uncontrollably until he can get to several church board members and tell them how wrong they have been. He promises God that he will change and he does. In this dramatized case, God appears to have broken His rule of "protecting His saints." How could God let such a thing happen to Betty? Couldn't He have "forced" her to listen? Did He decide to allow her suffering? Was this to teach a pastor and church board how to better exercise "protecting love." Would you have handled it differently?

Rule breaking should normally be reserved for God--after all He is the ultimate rule maker. Most of us are aware that breaking one rule often leads to breaking another, and the same is true of breaking a vow. This author believes that plenty of caution is needed before breaking any rule, and that extra special caution is necessary before breaking a vow. The person or persons involved should seek plenty of submission to authorities—both religious and civil. He or she should be in an ongoing submissive relationship to a healthy body of Christ.

Moreover, two or more witnesses are needed before anything can be firmly established (cf. Matthew 18:16, 2nd Corinthians 13:1 & 1st Timothy 5:19). This often takes a long period of time. One key point here is in regard to a "healthy" body of Christ. Such a fellowship must have a good handle on the rules and on Scriptural innovations about how to apply the rules—including the rule of love.

Also, this book about divorces in the Bible is likely to open up a lot of freedom for the "oppressed." However, oppression is not something to be exaggerated for the sake of getting one's own way. Again, other mature Christians need to be in agreement with the alleged complaint before any "tearing asunder" (or rule breaking) is undertaken.

To close out this introductory section, some further appetizers are offered by way of a list. This list gives most of the motivations for writing this book about *"Divorce as 'Required' by Scripture."* The issues within this list are covered at various lengths in the upcoming chapters. The list begins with the more important items and moves toward those of lesser importance:

1. Respect the intent of traditionalists
2. Reflect Bible "harmony" from Genesis to Revelation
3. Reason directly from Scripture
4. Return to Bible foundations...for divorce
5. Reclaim "Our Father's" love for underdogs
6. Remove the "oppression" of the marriage vow
7. Resurrect the "father's privilege" to break a vow
8. Reconstitute single parent "families"
9. Rebuke "proof text" prejudice, e.g. Rom 7:1ff
10. Reveal two "wills of God," i.e. perfect & permissive
11. Rely appropriately on Jewish perspective
12. Recognize the "martyr modification" impact
13. Recommend practical tests and solutions
14. Reinforce inductive study of Scripture

15. Renew "rapture-ready" effects, e.g. purification
16. Reduce complexities and related rationalizations
17. Restrict tendency toward unbridled freedom
18. Report (partially) on personal experience
19. React to questionable analysis of polls
20. Reverse overdone self-blame for divorce

Part I
Bible Bases

-1-

Serious Safeguards

Sunburn is painful. Why then do you suppose that so many people get sunburned so many times? One reason may be that the out-of-doors is so inviting and enjoyable that normal caution is pushed aside. Freedom from extra clothing is also a factor in how much of oneself gets sunburned. Another issue, in this new millennium, is the rate at which burning rays from the sun reach our skin. We are told that it happens faster than in previous generations. Today's parents therefore have to be more careful with their children. We want them to enjoy the sun, but we do not want them to be painfully burned from too much "freedom" in the sun. In the same way, this chapter about serious safeguards—for Scriptural divorce—is meant to prevent painful misuse of the freedom provided by seldom used Scriptures. These often forgotten Scriptures, and related principles, must be used with serious caution!

The word "Required" is used in this book with special safeguarding (and with some writer's privilege). Several Scriptures seem to "require" divorce but related principles must not be overlooked. When all the pertinent principles are applied, one will have a good case for applying the word "required." Otherwise, serious errors are likely.

The most often overlooked principle is that of the spiritual gift of martyrdom. It is frequently suggested, in an unwitting manner, by those who say to stay in a marriage no matter what happens. These folks usually have good intentions but the results of their simple rule are often quite hypocritical. Telling a battered wife to let him do it again may lead to her death, as a martyr because of the rule of "no matter what happens." She should never be *pushed* into such martyrdom. She may *choose* such martyrdom with help from trusted advisors but she should never be pushed into it. (Those who would so advise her should also be willing to prove that they have already risked their own lives for the cause of Christ.) Those spouses who properly choose the gift of martyrdom are welcome to risk being battered "for the cause." Divorce is not "required" for them. But those spouses without this gift may see divorce as "required."

On the other hand are those who say the grace of God covers almost any divorce. These folks "require" the rest of us to just let divorce happen as often as it does. Here too we have problems. The divorce initiator can probably escape most abuse and any other distasteful treatment. But what about the children? Will part of their personality be "martyred" against their wishes? Will they be better off, or not? How long will it take to find out? It is easy to see why serious cautions must be exercised for the good of all parties. This includes grandparents, other relatives, friends and neighbors.

Another matter for serious safeguarding is related to the fact that God *does change* His mind. He does it for proper cause. Jeremiah 18 tells us that God will specifically reverse his plan (for good or bad) if his people will reverse their path. But many Christians have memorized Numbers 23:19 where God is described as one who *does not change* His mind. Numbers 23:19 differs from Jeremiah 18 in that it is an over-arching description of God's general blessing upon His people.

A specific reversal by God is found in 1st Samuel 2:30, relating to a promise given to Eli. Another reversal by God, in a national way, is found in Deuteronomy 31. In verse 6 Moses tells the Israelites that God will never leave them nor forsake them, but in verse 17 God tells Moses that at a future time He will forsake them.

Psalm 33:11 indicates to us that God's *overall* purposes and plans stand forever, but many cases of *individual* change do occur in the Scriptures. (See also e.g. Ezekiel chapters 3 and 33, Jonah 3 & Zechariah 8.) The bottom line here is that God himself may support one marriage or another for a good number of years but withdraw His support when one or both spouses are too harmful for too long.

Mercy is another area to safeguard. James 2:13 tells us that those who will not show mercy will not receive mercy. The beatitudes echo this principle.

Refusal to allow for any divorce is unmerciful. Those who take such a stand are not too likely to receive mercy from the Lord in their day of need. Many church folks who currently cannot find mercy—might find it—if they would rethink their unmerciful position on divorce. On the other hand we should not show too much mercy, for that can turn grace into a license for sin.

Spouses in troubled marriages will likely need lots of "outside" help in trying to measure how well they have been applying mercy. Advisors must safeguard the process of establishing truth. They should not defend, or support, either spouse—without good amounts of firmly established information. This process can become much like a modern-day trial, taking many days or even weeks.

After months of examination in the famous O.J. Simpson case, was anyone on the jury (or in the media) able to say with certainty that he did, or did not, commit that murder? The same principle applies to most accusations in most cases of divorce. Unless eyewitnesses are available, who are able to independently corroborate each other, the full truth may never be known.

God knew this principle a long time ago when He required two or more witnesses for establishing truth. See Deuteronomy 19:15, Matthew 18:16, 2nd Corinthians 13:1 and 1st Timothy 5:19. This serious principle from

Scripture is expanded in Acts 25:16. Here the accused is given opportunity to face his accusers and to defend himself.

Church officials need to take the above texts serious. How can we even dare to assume any guilt, or innocence, until the standards of God are met in our examination of "the facts?" Yes, this safeguard is challenging, but without meeting it, we must admit that we just do not know enough to side with either party. Unless these standards are met, we basically must leave the matter in God's hands. When and if He is ready to reveal the story-behind-the-story, we will know it. Only then can we make equitable judgments. Until then much of what happens is up to the separating and/or divorcing parties. Our main job is to love and guide with gentleness and humility, to whatever degree we are allowed....

Lastly for now is the safeguard for the victim of the hardhearted spouse. In Deuteronomy 24:1-4, Moses rule from God was for those whose hearts were hard. In many cases of divorce, hearts have already been hardened and will not soften any time soon. Therefore church officials and friends can do little more than pray and love and hope. We are not likely to ever know for sure who started the trouble, who caused the trouble to increase, who is unable or unwilling to forgive at the deepest levels, who is most responsible before God for the trouble, who is best able to solve the trouble, or even if the trouble can be solved in such a way to make the marriage truly Christian. We can warn divorcing parties of the seriousness of their actions. We can exhort them to tell their counselors the whole truth. We can plead with them on behalf of any children involved and warn them specifically about the risk of sinning against their children. But ultimately it is the hardhearted spouse(s) who must change—to the ways of God.

In some divorce cases only one spouse has a hard heart. If the hard-hearted spouse is determined to get a divorce, the Deuteronomy provision can be a gift to the one who is not hardened. Jesus did not recommend Deuteronomy 24 but neither did he do away with it. He reminds us of the higher road but he does not remove the safety net for victims of hard-heartedness. Many times the one with the hard heart unwittingly rescues his/her victim by initiating a divorce "against" him/her. The church should be cautious about trying to prevent such a rescue--it might just be a gift from God. He is often so serious about protecting one of his victimized children—that He causes (or allows) a divorce.

Those persons who would safeguard both sides of the serious issues in this book are likely to be viewed as pioneers. Successful pioneers are usually serious and cautious—as well as adventuresome. The writer of this book has tried to be serious and cautious. I believe that failure to put forward the pioneering interpretations of this book might be a sin of omission. I also accept the serious possibility of discipline or punishment from God for encouraging any unnecessary divorce. In any case, this book does seem to be needed—since so many folks have not heard much about *"Divorce as 'Required' by Scripture."*

-2-

Divorce, the 11th Commandment?

In regard to being close to the Ten Commandments, divorce is almost "the eleventh." The title for this chapter is purposely provocative to make that point. You can find God's first requirement for divorce almost immediately after the Ten Commandments. The Big Ten are in Exodus chapter 20 and divorce is at the beginning of chapter 21. Only one set of regulations (about altars) is between the "Big Ten" and divorce. Since Jesus did away with those earthen altars, we could almost call divorce "the 11th Commandment." Actually the Ten Commandments are in a class by themselves, having been written by the finger of God. There are about 600 other laws, rules, and ordinances recorded by Moses, but none can accurately be labeled as "the 11th Commandment."

How then is it that many millions of believers miss the many divorces in Exodus chapter 21? Perhaps the main reason is that the word "divorce" is not directly used in the rule of law being addressed in verses one thru six. Another reason is that many believers today use mostly the New Testament, and forget about the Old. Another reason is the ingrained teaching about upholding traditional marriages in regard to their permanence. This teaching is to be admired, and should be followed, but not when it does considerably more harm than good.

Harm and good were apparently in view when God inspired Moses to address Hebrew servitude, at the beginning of Exodus chapter 21. Let's review that issue:

1. a Hebrew servant was to be set free after six years,
2. if he came alone, he left alone,
3. if he came with a wife, she too left with him,
4. if the master gave him a wife, he could not take her with him, even if she bore him children -UNLESS
5. the servant would state that he LOVED:
    a. his master, and
    b. his wife, and
    c. their children
6. the servant would also state that he did not want to go free (but would serve the master for life).

Divorce occurred at step number four. The servant was required to leave without his new wife and their children UNLESS LOVE had entered the picture. Notice also the order of his new loves, i.e. master, then wife, and finally children.

The text also suggests that the servant had to convince the judge(s) of his sincerity. Otherwise he was to be discharged and his wife & children stayed with the master. This amounted to a divorce, even though there is no mention of a certificate of divorcement. The servant and the wife he had been given had become one flesh. They were married, and they had children to prove it. But this marriage was doomed unless something special had also become a part of it. That special thing, needed to make their marriage "permanent," was LOVE.

The kind of love at issue was a three-way love. First was the love of his job so that he would do a good job there. Second was his love for his wife and third were the children. Loves two & three would mean using his "income" for the good purpose of raising a family.

God had said for man to be fruitful and to multiply. A passing note here is that such fruitfulness meant the joining of flesh. The Bible frequently refers to marriage as the joining of flesh, see Genesis 2:24, Matthew 19:5, 1st Corinthians 6:16, and Ephesians 5:31.

The servant's three-way love was apparently very important to God in terms of what kind of marriage is worth keeping. One could easily imagine that going before the judges could backfire if the servant's wife did not confirm her belief in her husband's love. Perhaps the children were in the courtroom as well, and maybe one would testify. A good judge could also find other ways to discover from the other children whether they had a love relationship with their "servant-dad."

If the servant failed the test for three-way love, it was the rule of God that he was to leave. God apparently did not want that wife and children to have such a man for a husband or father. Better to be a single mother, at least for awhile, than to have an unloving man in the family.

It is also worth noting here some of the reasons that a Hebrew man found himself in servitude. He may have been just plain lazy. He may have lived beyond his means and gotten into so much debt that servitude was his only answer. He may have had an unteachable spirit and therefore no useful skill for producing enough money to make a living. He may have gotten himself into some wrongful civil behavior that required repayment—beyond what he had. He may even have been working off some debt for his parent(s).

Regardless of the reason, such a servant would not make a good husband & father until he had a heart change. It would appear that the master gave him a very good second chance and that to "blow it," meant divorce. Some lessons in life can only be learned the hard way.

By mathematical extrapolation, one could easily estimate that the rule of God in Exodus 21 could have totaled over 50,000 "servant divorces" per generation. They were not labeled as divorces but that is still what occurred. There were about six million Jews within the twelve tribes. Suppose that only two men out of a hundred were involved in "servant divorce," and that men made up slightly less than half of the population

(6,000,000 X 45% = 2,700,000; 2,700,000 X .02 = 54,000). Round these down to 50,000 and multiply times about 30 generations—from Exodus 21 to the time of Christ--and we find well over one million such divorces! Perhaps these divorces are one major reason why the issues surrounding "servant divorce" followed so closely on the heels of the Ten Commandments.

Some astute readers may now be thinking about the popular saying, "God hates divorce." Many Christian leaders, declare with "stained-glass" voice, that Gawwdd despises divorce! They find support for this bellowing near the end of the Old Testament, in Malachi 2:16.

But let's ask ourselves one important question. If it is true that God hates divorce, then why did He require servant divorces, per Exodus 21? And why did He Himself divorce Israel (Jeremiah 3:8)? This writer believes that God does not hate divorce....

Believers who think that He does (hate divorce) will be tempted to come up with some other way to describe what happened in Exodus 21:1-6. They may even try to say that the servant was not really married because there is no record of a ceremony. Such believers should take note that no ceremony is recorded for Isaac.

Genesis 24:67, in the NIV, reports that Isaac took Rebecca into his mother's tent and married her. His mother, Sarah, had already passed away; so, her tent was probably empty. This Scripture still says that Isaac "married" Rebecca, and that she became his wife. Had not the Hebrew servant done the same thing? Were there not children to prove the "marriage?"

There is another answer to this apparent dilemma. The King James Version says in Malachi 2:16 that God hateth "putting away." Is divorce the same as "putting away?" Some, like Reverend Guy Duty (*Divorce & Remarriage*), say it is the same. But this author believes that they are not the same, and that Duty's "documentation" is in error. Personal research and a recent book by Reverend Walter Callison show that divorce is quite different from "putting away." (In order to highlight that difference, the term "putting away," or "put away," will be enclosed in quotations for most of the rest of this book.)

Brother Callison has no ax to grind and no divorce in his family. He is a retired Baptist pastor and simply set about resolving the issue at hand by looking into the Greek and Hebrew languages. He looked deep and wide, only to discover and prove the difference between divorce and "put away." Much more is to be said about this later.

For now, in our New Testament (Greek) times, it should suffice to say that divorce is from the Greek word apostasion. It has a Strong's Concordance number 647. "Put away" is from the Greek word apoluo, with a different Strong's number, 630. Both begin with "apo" but their ends tell a different story. One might compare these two words with the colors of red and pink. And note that a deep pink can easily be described as pale red. However pink is not red, and red is not pink.

In Old Testament times (and New), to "put away" one's wife meant *to separate* from her. A vengeful Hebrew husband would also refuse to give her *a bill of divorcement* as required by Moses in Deuteronomy 24. In any number of these vengeful cases, it is presumed that the husband simply sent her out of the house to fend for herself. She would not be able to remarry, but he often took a second wife, or concubine.

Today we often hear that a husband, or wife, has "cut off" the opposite spouse (from sexual relations, etc.) They are still married but in name only. They may or may not continue to live in the same residence—but one has "put away" the other.

Divorce on the other hand, means just that. It is interesting to note that the King James Version has it right in the Greek (New Testament) every time except once. The New International Version has it wrong every time.

We are nevertheless thankful for how the NIV got the sixth commandment (Old Testament) right with saying that *murder* is forbidden. The KJV says that *killing* is forbidden. Both versions are excellent and together they become superior. Note also that the NIV is not alone among the many modern translations, in regard to mistranslating "put away."

Some killing is murder but some is not. Sometimes "putting away," or separating, ends in divorce but often it does not. Deep pink is the same as light red—but pink is not red. If a driver of a car runs over a child who just ran out from between two parked cars, he is not a murderer. He *has killed* but he *has not murdered.*

A man who hates his boss and purposely runs over him with a forklift has killed him, and murdered him. Word choice does make a difference. It's the same with the Greek words, and Hebrew words, for "put away" and divorce. This writer agrees with Callison that God hated it when a man "put away" his wife (without the required bill of divorcement). Malachi 2:16 then is no longer a good proof for how God "obviously" hates divorce. How could he hate what He requires?

Other Scriptures, which prove that God requires divorce, are found in both the Old Testament and the New Testament. Several of these texts will be given thorough attention in upcoming chapters. One purpose of this book is to show an undeniable pattern of divorces "required" in the Scriptures. This pattern by itself should be enough to prove the title of this book but other, strong support can also be found in the original languages. The upcoming chapter entitled '*Converted by Callison*' gives the basics of original language support for "divorce" versus "put away."

However, before ending this chapter, let's list some principles and applications that can be taken from it. Appropriate caution must be used with such listings due to the main source, i.e. Exodus 21. This text and others from the Old Testament are somewhat impacted by New Testament teachings. A more thorough discussion of those impacts will be given when the New Testament teachings are presented. (The main texts for this book are presented in the same order as found in the Bible.)

Principles Perceived

1. Divorce was begun by God, as early as Exodus 21.

2. Hebrew servitude implied further character flaws.

3. Importance of a man's love for work, wife & children.

4. Use of judges to evaluate a man's (three) loves.

5. Family gained during servitude must be loved, or lost.

6. God prefers single motherhood more than marriage "permanence" if the man does not love as he should...

7. Even though the word divorce is not used in Ex. 21, the result over time could still be millions of divorces

8. Marriage, in the Hebrew, is the joining of flesh

9. Divorce is different from "put away."

10. A good memory "hook" for finding divorce in the Bible is to look right after the Ten Commandments...

Applications Advised

1. Accept Exodus 21:1-6 as one foundation for proving that God sometimes ordains divorce.

2. Consider divorce when a man continues in not loving his wife & children and the job that supports them all.

3. Accept single motherhood (for a while) after being married to an unloving man for more than six years.

4. Learn the difference between divorce, and "put away," as used in various Bible versions, e.g. Good News Bible, King James Version, New King James, New American Standard, New International Version, etc.

5. Use both the KJV and the NIV when studying divorce and "put away" texts (the KJV is usually right, the NIV and other modern translations usually are not).

6. Allow more than one chance at marriage (the children of a sent away servant would still need a father, and his ex-wife would still need a husband—hopefully one with the LOVE solution.

7. Keep in mind that Jesus recognized five marriages by one woman—not one marriage and four adulteries (see John 4:18).

Chapter Closing Caution -- Please remember those Serious Safeguards from chapter one. Some of the applications advised above would require at least two of them: (1) being submissive to the body of Christ so as to lower the risk of subjective decision-making, and (2) having two or more cross-examinable witnesses for establishing "facts."

-3-

Converted by Callison

Reverend Walter Callison wrote an article in 1986 for a magazine called *Your Church.* It appeared in the May/June issue (pp. 18-23). This article was a perfect answer to some years of prayer by my mother & dad. They had been praying for me to give up the celibate lifestyle, temporary and self-imposed as it was. Loving parents and son would periodically examine the issue, due to my having once been "happily" married for about seventeen years. One-day mother sent the Callison article to me, and God used it to convert my thinking and lifestyle. May there be millions more who are converted by Callison's work.

Rev. Callison is now also author Callison. Recently (2002), his book entitled *Divorce, A Gift of God's Love* was published. It is available at Amazon.com, or by contacting him: wcallison@cox.net. It should again be noted that Callison has never been divorced and has no divorce in his family. He simply wanted to solve the apparent difficulties in regard to divorce, versus "put away." The latter term being used in the King James Version of the Bible and the former being used in most modern translations. It is my fervent hope that his book, and others in the same genre, will be used to convert the thinking of some famous scholars. Perhaps then the church will get over its legalistic way of handling so many divorces and remarriages.

Before going into Callison's new book, it should be worthwhile to give some personal testimony. This will help show why it was so important to be converted by God, through that old article by Callison.

For much of the last century, my denomination had forbidden remarriage. Their Manual of Doctrine said that ministers were not permitted to perform a marriage ceremony if either party had a former spouse living. (One might wonder how many homicides were considered due to this legalistic rule.) Thank God that the leaders did finally change that harsh rule. It had been there for a good purpose, i.e. to uphold the permanence of marriage. However, it was written much too tightly and had to go. By the way, some other denominations still have the same old rule, or a policy, that achieves the same result.

The denomination referenced above has been my home from 1980 until now, and it has otherwise been a very good home. My one, previous denomination had been a rather liberal, mainliner. From birth to age twenty-five, my religion seemed quite satisfactory. Then things began to change.... And after five more years of not finding that close walk with the Spirit of Jesus, my denominational affiliation needed to be changed. After more years of prayer and soul-searching, my heart led me away from that noticeably liberal and lukewarm denomination, into a lively but occasionally legalistic one.

My "conversion" to a conservative denomination worked out rather well, for the most part. One issue that came up right away was my status of being separated (and later divorced) from the wife of my youth. My prayer partners helped me into the Hosea vision as posited by Bill Gothard. This helped keep me single for about seven years. During that time, an old promise to God, about going to seminary, was fulfilled. This meant coercing upon myself a celibate lifestyle. The Lord gets most of the credit for this and the successful completion of a Master of Divinity degree. My new church then also licensed me as a minister.

During those years, my church was testing the waters a bit in regard to a divorced minister. Guess who became one of their guinea pigs? This experience gave many positive moments and some negative ones. The article by Walter Callison became even more important as it helped convert the thinking of my pastor. He was very good with the Greek and quickly agreed with Callison's article. What a relief to him and me. He tried to convert some other church leaders but did not have much success.

You see, in a conservative denomination, a good article about the Greek meanings is helpful but...there needs to be a book. And then some other books, that at least agree with this "new teaching" about divorce vs. "put away." There is so much at stake!

Meanwhile my ex-wife finally legalized her marriage to one of my former "friends." This man was by then legally divorced from his *devoted* wife. She lived alone until she died. A number of folks concluded that she died, younger than expected, due largely to a broken heart. Lack of *devotion* enabled my first wife to initiate the divorce that broke our marriage. (Also, my former "friend" was of that liberal denomination).

Both of these broken families had children. Each had one daughter with the same name, Kimberly. About twenty years later my gifted, but estranged, daughter Kimberly died from drowning, apparently after jumping off a bridge. Until then, she seemed to have it all, i.e. good job, successful husband, new house, and a cherished and wonderful son. Was there trouble in her marriage? Could her real dad have helped?

My hope in telling you this part of the story is that your might see the weight attached to converting my thinking about divorce and remarriage. On many occasions, love for my four children almost stopped my heart from beating. This was because they were suffering so much, and so unknowingly—having lost sight of "normal." Often, it became almost unbearable to see the direction they were taking. Most of my seven years of celibacy was for them—that they would be restored to normalcy. There was so much at stake! Was Callison correct? Or, would another seven years of celibacy have yielded the once hoped-for results?

These questions gave me plenty of passion to search the entire Bible again and again. (It is my practice to read every word of it, from Genesis one to Revelation twenty-two, every year. This has been going on for well over twenty years.) Did the Bible support my church entirely? Or, does the Bible support both the permanence of marriage and second chances for those who are divorced. Especially important was the question, "What about those who are the victim of an unwanted divorce?" (My divorce was against my wishes...but Pennsylvania was a "No-Fault" state...and there was essentially no way to stop the divorce.)

My sin should now be confessed in regard to my first marriage, and how it began. At least three sins were involved: (1) the failure to ask the Lord whether to get married, (2) the failure to ask Him who was a good person to marry, and (3) the failure to ask Him when might be a good age to marry? Aside from these major errors and a couple of sinful stumbles, my first marriage had been well above average. We often took those marital tests in Reader's Digest and scored high.

But the fullness of the Holy Spirit was not there. One day He came, and that was good, but He came with a sword. Little by little, my faith got deeper but hers waned. She found someone else who was into church a little. . .but just a little. I wish that I had been into church, a lot, when we had first met. Important Spiritual matters would likely have been settled then, one way or the other. And precious children would not have been so damaged.

The article by Callison would probably not ever have been needed. This however points to a huge blind spot in most churches. Churches are strong for family, and that is wonderful. The down side is that churches do not know much about what to do with broken families.

Most churches properly excel at holding families together. Callison, and others like him, are needed when families are broken. This is especially true in conservative circles. Conservatives rightly require a model directly from the Bible. My Bible-based "model" is within the pages of this book. It is founded upon many passages, which add up to solid proof for *"Divorce as 'Required' by Scripture."*

Brother Callison's article and book delve more directly into poorly translated words, in both the Hebrew and Greek. Many of his major findings are now listed to help convince the reader that his solution is from God.

1. The Hebrew word for divorce is *keriythuwth;* this word is used in Jeremiah 3:8—meaning legalized divorce as we think of today.

2. The (usual) Hebrew word for "put away" is *shalach;* this word is used in Malachi 2:16 -meaning to send away (or "put away"). Callison draws

attention to how the Jewish man would do this and not give the bill of divorcement required by Moses. My research also indicates that some such periods of *shalach* would have been temporary. In these latter cases, there was no need for the bill of divorcement.

3. Benita Gayle-Almeleh of the American Jewish Committee once estimated at least 35,000 Jewish women in America to be in marital limbo. Their civilly divorced husbands would not grant a religious divorce (as required in Deuteronomy 24). These women were therefore "put away," but could not remarry. (They were not given a Jewish "get." The word "get" refers to a bill of divorce signed by their respective husbands.)

4. The Greek word for divorce is *apostasion;* it is used in Matthew 5:31 in regard to the writing of divorcement, or certificate of divorce, (and needs no interpretation).

5. The Greek word for separation is *apoluo;* it is used by Jesus eleven times in passages about divorce and remarriage, e.g. Matthew 19:9. In each passage, He opposed apoluo ("put away"). He never opposed apostasion (divorce writ)—it was required by the law.

6. Ten out of those eleven times, the King James Version translated apoluo as "put away," but in one instance the KJV made apoluo to say divorce.

This occurred at the end of Matthew 5:31-32, and was an error.

7. Apoluo is used sixty-nine (69) times in the New Testament. There is only one time when it was translated "divorce" by the KJV—at the end of Mt 5:32. This amounts to sure evidence that the word "divorceth," in the KJV (at the end of Mt 5:32) was an error.

8. That error in the 1611 KJV was corrected. In 1901, the very literal American Standard Version, always made apoluo to say, "put away." And this American Standard Version was following a previous correction—the KJV Revision of 1881-85.

9. One of our modern translations has kept a clear and accurate difference between divorce and "put away," i.e. Eerdman's *The New Testament, An Expanded Translation* by Moody Bible School Professor, Kenneth S. Wuest. Wuest always translates apoluo as dismiss, or "put away," and he consistently states apostasion as divorce.

10. Callison's bibliography for his findings include: *A Greek-English Lexicon,* Arndt-Gingrich; *The Life and Works of Josephus,* Whiston; *Langenscheidt Pocket Hebrew Dictionary,* Langenscheidt; *Analytical Hebrew and Chaldee Lexicon,* Benjamin Davidson; *Holy Bible,* American Standard Version; *Holy Bible,* King James Version; *The Greek New Testament,* United Bible Societies; *A Concise Greek-English*

Dictionary of the New Testament, Newman; *Strong's Exhaustive Concordance,* Strong; *The New World,* Dana; *Holy Bible,* Revised Standard Version; *Introducing the Bible,* Barclay; *The Broadman Bible Commentary,* Stagg; *For This Day,* Phillips; *Wayward Bus,* Steinbeck; and *The New Testament, An Expanded Translation,* Wuest; *Holy Bible From The Ancient Eastern Text (George M. Lamsa's Translation From The Aramaic Of The Peshitta),* Lamsa; Malachi: *Rekindling The Fires Of Faith,* Kelley.

Brother Callison may not have a lot of letters behind his name but his work may well have exceeded that of many scholars, with lots of degrees. It would appear that some scholars have missed the forest due to honing in on their particular tree(s).

Callison's work was used by the good Lord in 1986 to convert my thinking. His recent book helped stir my passion to write my own book. There are not a lot of letters behind my name but the forest view of the entire Bible convinces me that there are many divorces "required" by the Scriptures. It is my hope that many readers will also be convinced by Callison's approach, and the approach of this writer.

One more approach seems especially important to mention just now. Good words to describe it include: pastoral, reasonable, and gracious. This approach was taken by Larry Richards in 1981—in his book *"Remarriage: A Healing Gift from God."* Richard's book came close to getting me out of my celibacy but it was not quite enough for those who say, "Show it to me directly in the Scriptures." These folks admired Richards for his many scholarly works. The college of my own denomination has many of Richards' textbooks in their library. However, even though my peer group would go along with Richards, they would not embrace or highly recommend his approach. Someone planning to pastor for them would have an uphill battle if he were remarried. Richards' overall approach was the best ever, to me. The problem was my need and the need of my peers to see it proven easily and directly in the Scriptures. A further problem to me was the need to see remarriage as approved by God in a topical overview of the entire Bible. This would make the case one "worth dying for."

A three-way approach would give me the confidence to lay aside all fears, concerns and worry about standing before Jesus on Judgment Day. It would enable me also to face my daughter Kimberly someday in Heaven with a clear conscience (and three other children in the meantime). Seven years of coerced celibacy was almost enough. Their mother's remarriage to a former friend was almost enough. But my bottom line on "enough" became a three-way approach described below:

- Callison's heart as a pastor, and his translation specificity, and his dogged investigative work.

- Richards' pastoral mindedness, along with his gracious and sound reasoning. Of course Richards' wide acceptance as a highly respected Christian author helps immensely.

- Lastly, is the topical approach, from Genesis to Revelation—as given in this book.

As the chapter ends, we again have some principles, applications, and cautions. Such highlighting of important issues is planned for each chapter in this book, except when deemed unnecessary.

Principles Perceived

1. Bible scholars are often worth their weight in gold but occasionally they miss the forest for the trees.

2. A good investigator, like Walter Callison, can sometimes find that which almost everyone else has missed.

3. The pastoral (and loving) approach, like that of Richards and Callison, is usually correct—because the letter of the law kills but the Spirit gives life.

4. The greater the importance of a decision, the more need there is to have greater evidence for making that decision.

5. Weighty decisions should also be influenced by more than one methodology.

Applications Advised

1. Learn to appreciate each (and every) tree in the forest of Scriptures for what it is worth.

2. Remember also to look at the whole forest, for whatever patterns can be observed from a distance.

3. Be submissive to good authority, e.g. experience, honesty, logic, scholarship, Spirituality, wisdom, etc.

Chapter Closing Caution

My three-way approach to solving questions about divorce and remarriage is not being held up as the ultimate approach. There may well be others that are as good or better.

-4-

Ezra's "Evictions"

The next stop in our topical survey of divorces in the Bible is the Book of Ezra. He is described in Ezra 7:6 as a scribe. Scribes were well versed in the law (of Moses) and many were also teachers of the law. Ezra was written more than 500 years before Christ and about 1000 years after the Ten Commandments. The Israelites had been in captivity for seventy years in Babylon and a remnant was returning to Jerusalem.

The main point of interest about divorces occurs in chapters nine and ten, the last two chapters of Ezra. A summary of those chapters is now enumerated:

1. Jewish leaders told Ezra that the Israelites had been marrying non-Israelites; even some priests & Levites had intermarried with foreigners.

2. Ezra was appalled; he tore his clothes and pulled his hair and beard. Also, the people trembled....

3. Ezra prayed, and confessed the sin of the people; many Israelites were present (men, women & children).

4. A man named Shecaniah spoke up, saying that there was hope, namely in the "putting away" or sending away of the wives who were not Israelites. (Ezra 10:3, 19)

5. Shecaniah specifically said that this solution should be accomplished according to the Law (of Moses).

6. Ezra got the leaders and the Israelites to agree with what Shecaniah had proposed....

7. Ezra went away for fasting from food and water. On the third day, the people gathered in Jerusalem. It was a rainy day.

8. Ezra charged the people with intermarriage, told them to confess this sin to God, and to do His will—by separating themselves from their foreign wives.

9. The people agreed with Ezra and then the investigation of cases took place. It is likely that some foreigners had already become "Jewish," and would not have to leave. It is also possible that some financial settlement took place.

10. Three months later, over one hundred cases had been settled: 17 priests, 10 Levites, 3 gatekeepers, and 84 others. These are named at the end of the Book of Ezra.

11. Tragically, the last detail of Ezra (10:44) is that some of these men with foreign wives...also had children.

Much more could be written about Ezra. More, related information is found in Nehemiah, a companion book to Ezra. Readers are encouraged to study Ezra and Nehemiah for deeper understandings. Part of my study included a check of over a dozen Bible translations, in regard to that word divorce. Only one used it; the rest say send away, put away, get rid of, etc. The Hebrew word used here is neither *shalach* nor *keriythuwth.* It is *yatsa*—meaning get away, "put away," or send with commandment (Strong's #3318). "With commandment," likely included the certificate of divorce—as supported at the end of Ezra 10:3. (This support is missing in Ex. 21:4, where *yatsa* is also used.)

This chapter on Ezra might be the best place to say something about Bible euphemisms. A euphemism is a substitute word that tones down, or softens, an otherwise strong word. Two examples should help make this clear:

a. Sexual Intercourse, is a term that does not appear in any well-known Bible. What we read instead is that Adam "knew" his wife, or that he "lay" with her (Genesis 4:1 & 4:25). Compare also that Joseph "knew" not his wife, or had no "union" with Mary, until after Jesus was born (Matthew 1:25).

b. Dead, is another term that is toned down, or softened, by Jesus himself (John 11:11-15). John records Jesus first saying that Lazarus had fallen asleep. The disciples wrongly thought that Jesus meant normal sleep. Jesus then told them plainly, or more directly, that Lazarus was dead.

In the same way, the word divorce is not used in the Book of Ezra. However the context easily proves that divorce is what happened. Various translations soften the occurrences of divorce with different terms, even as the Hebrew did the same thing. Such softening does not change what happened. It simply tells the same story in a kinder and gentler way.

Failure to recognize this pattern in Ezra, or elsewhere, is to fail to properly interpret the Bible. Such failure actually takes away from what the Bible is saying. In the Book of Revelation, near the very end, we are warned not to take away from what the Bible is saying. It is a sin that carries heavy penalties, especially when done knowingly and intentionally.

It seems to me that a lot of Bible "students" are in serious trouble with God for how they have missed this issue of divorce. Some even go so far as to use Malachi 2:16 to show that Ezra went against the will of God. It is almost ridiculous to use one word in Malachi to overcome an entire context, and the Law of Moses, as used in Ezra.

One easy way to compare those "troublesome events" in Ezra is to consider today's apartment renters. If they do not pay their rent, they break their contract. The Israelites had also broken their contract with God.

Folks who do not pay their rent can be "evicted," under the laws of our country. Ezra used the Law of God to "evict" those women who were not true blue Jews. They were "evicted" out of their marriages. In the same way that an apartment "eviction" ends the contract between a landlord and tenant, a divorce ends the marriage between a husband and wife. Thus we have a memorable & telling title for this chapter, i.e. *Ezra's "Evictions."*

Part of my writing plan is to keep this book short and to the point, whenever possible. Therefore, we can now go directly to principles, applications, and cautions.

Principles Perceived

1. God's chosen people were not allowed to intermarry with non-Israelites, according to the Law of Moses. See Deuteronomy 7:3, and Exodus 34:15-16.

2. Ezra had encountered a number of Israelites who had gone against the Law, by marrying non-Israelites.

3. Only one solution was available in those Old Testament times, i.e. divorce.

4. Even though the word "divorce" is not used, it is a proper interpretation for at least four reasons:

a. The context proves that divorce did happened,

b. Shecaniah stated that the sending away must be accomplished in accordance with the Law.

c. The Law required a written bill of divorce.

d. This Law (of Moses) is found in Deuteronomy 24:1-4. The Hebrew word used there is a sure word for divorce, i.e. keriythuwth.

5. The Scriptural practices of prayer and fasting, along with confession, were clearly involved.

6. The answers to prayer agreed with the written word.

7. Keeping the Israelite nation "pure," was more important than keeping an impure marriage together. It was even more important than seeing the children of those marriages continue to have their biological father and mother.

8. The Israelite people and many of their leaders had apparently not "learned their lesson" during their 70 year exile. They fell quickly back into sin, despite the punishment of being away from home for so long. This probably added to God's "need" of sending away those foreign women—who would further water down the faith of their weak husbands.

9. Judgments about divorce take time for plenty of investigation by those who have good knowledge of the circumstances.

10. The writer of Ezra may have been so broken hearted about those children that he could write no more after mentioning them.

<u>*Applications Advised*</u>

1. Christians should not marry those who are not Christian. This is verified in 2nd Corinthians 6:14.

2. Jews should not marry those who are not Jewish. Jesus did not do away with any of their Law. See Matthew 5:17-18.

3. Under certain conditions, divorce must occur in order to meet the requirements of God. Please note that the New Testament has somewhat changed this—as will be highlighted in the cautions.... Such divorces must be allowed at all levels, i.e. for those of high office such as priest or for those with no office.

4. Under certain circumstances, children may be taken away from an unbelieving parent, even if their chance of seeing that parent may be lost forever. One key issue here is the child's need to be reared in the things of God. Another key issue is whether the believing parent already has a viable relationship with the child.

5. Considerable confession, along with prayer and fasting should always accompany these weighty decisions.

6. The decisions reached must be in agreement with Scriptural models.

7. Christians who fall back into carnal ways may also be considered as unworthy for the job of parenting if their backsliding continues too far for too long a period of time.

8. When things get bad, as they were in Ezra's time, we must face the possibility that there is not much hope for the children of parents who intentionally disobey God.

Chapter Closing Cautions

1. Please—Fully Consider this First Caution!! The Ezra type of divorce had one primary cause: that was an unbelieving wife. In the New Testament, an unbelieving wife is not necessarily a reason for divorce. The same is true if an unbelieving husband is married to a believing wife. The decision making point in the New Testament is found in 1st Corinthians 7:12-15. The decision making point is whether the unbeliever is willing to live peaceably with the believer. If he or she is willing to live peaceably, then divorce is not needed. More is to be said about this later....

2. Remember that nothing shall be "established" except on the testimony of two or more witnesses. They must also be agreeable to cross-examination.

3. Some Christians are so carnal for so long that even Jesus can give up on them. Refer here to the seven letters to the churches in chapters two and three of Revelation. Also take note that not long after Ezra's time, God quit sending prophets to the Israelites; He had "given up" on that generation.

-5-

Wrestling with Wisdom

What about wisdom, in the Bible? Is there some place where one can usually find a lot of that? Yes, many sources state that the Books of Job, Psalms, Proverbs, and Ecclesiastes are "Wisdom Literature." Wisdom found in these books is often proverbial and general in nature. This means that sometimes one has to wrestle with what it means, when it applies, and to whom it is addressed.

Near the middle of the preceding chapter, we encountered a need to wrestle with "wisdom" from Malachi. Some Bible students use Malachi 2:16 to wiggle out of the evictions-by-divorce in Ezra chapters 9 & 10. They say that Malachi proves God's hatred of divorce. They then conclude that Ezra's evictions did not include a certificate of divorce (and its allowance to remarry). And even if there were certificates, Ezra was against the will of God—as shown by Malachi. But is their *wisdom* worthy?

Bible translations of Malachi 2:16 obviously disagree in stating *divorce*, or *"put away."* Worthy wisdom would say to let the strength of context in Ezra prove the sending away and the certificate of divorce. Then let Malachi stand within its own context, and its own translation(s). As we have already stated, God does not hate divorce, but God does hate "putting away." There is a huge difference between these two actions. This is just one important proof of the need to wrestle with wisdom.

Another proof comes from a Sunday School class in our church. One Sunday they got into debate about whether divorce and remarriage is allowed by the Bible. One side strongly supported marriage permanence by using Romans 7:1-3. This is a popular passage for supporting marriage permanence. The claim is something to the effect that marriages are "made in Heaven," and that only Heaven can break them. A county judge can grant a divorce decree to somebody but the couple is still married in God's eyes. This thinking goes against Deuteronomy 24. It also will not align with Jesus' recognition of the Samaritan woman who had had five husbands. Was she still married to five, in the eyes of God? Obviously not, because that would show God to be approving polygamy. If we submit to the county court (house) for obtaining a marriage license, why don't we submit when that same courthouse issues a divorce decree?

An amusing ending, to the debate in that class, is worth mentioning. The key text was that a married woman is bound to her husband for as long as he is alive.

An "uneducated" class member came to a truly wise conclusion. She said that the man in Romans 7:2 can no longer be called a husband—if he was divorced from his wife. So whether her Ex-husband lives, or dies, is of no concern in regard to a divorced woman getting remarried. Romans 7:2 does not "bind" a woman to her ex-husband!

Psalms 33:11 states that God's purposes and plans stand forever. However the methods He uses to achieve his purposes and plans can and do change. One sterling example is the contrast between King David and The Son of David. Jesus Christ was often called the Son of David, but He was "extremely" different from David in at least one area. Jesus killed no one; in fact, He died for the millions who would believe in Him. King David was given credit for killing tens of thousands. King David is spoken of highly, in Acts 13:22, as a man after God's own heart. Was Jesus not a man after God's own heart? Yes, of course, but his methods were "extremely" different. The plans and purposes of God had not changed. However, His method of achieving His plan was changed from the way He used David *to get rid of evil people*, to the way Christ was used *to pay for the sins of evil people.*

Some serious wrestling has to be done in regard to David and Jesus, in order to see how both can be Bible heroes. Killing for God, made some heroes in the Old Testament but not in the New. In the New Testatment, heroes are made by dying for God, and others....

In the same way, a similar comparison can be repeated from the last chapter. Divorce in Ezra's day was initiated by believers against unbelievers. On the other hand, divorce in the New Testament is not initiated by a believer against an unbeliever, if the unbeliever is willing to live peaceably with the believer (1st Cor. 7:12-13; 15-16). Has God's overall plan changed? No, but in the Church Age, He has apparently decided that believers should be able to stay strong in their faith, even if married to an unbeliever.... One key issue here is that the Holy Spirit was not poured out onto all flesh until the Church Age.

So what good does it do to wrestle with such issues? Much good can be accomplished if lessons learned are applied to other challenging issues. One of those challenging issues is, of course, divorce. So let's consider some of what we've been over just now and take it to Proverbs.

Proverbs 30:21-23 is the next place where this writer finds *"Divorce as 'Required' by Scripture."* Here is a summary of those verses:

1. There are four things that cause this world to tremble.

    a. a servant taking over a kingship
    b. an overfed fool
    c. a wife who is not loved (by her husband)
    d. a maid who overtakes her mistress

2. God's world will not allow these things to continue.

My focus, of course, is on the wife who is not loved by her husband. Modern translations of the Bible do fairly well with this one, especially the New International Version. Older versions do poorly. As one might therefore guess, several commentaries are questionable here. One can also find some evidence of male chauvinism. So let's run with the NIV, as being closest to the Hebrew, and build from there.

Principles Perceived

1. God's earthly creation is shaken when a married woman is not loved by her husband. If her husband will not love her, God's protective love is likely to rescue her from him. (See also 1st Corinthians 13: verse 7 & 8, NIV.)

2. God's earthly world will not allow a wife to be unloved for too long a period of time. In Exodus 21, the time could not exceed six years. This was somewhat by coincidence—as the Hebrew servant had to be freed in the seventh year. Only his love for his wife could enable him to keep her—past six years.

3. Just as the king would take back his throne from a servant, and just as a mistress would get rid of an overpowering maid, an unloved wife will have her problem solved.

4. The problem of the unloved wife has at least three potential solutions:

   a. A changed husband who would love his wife.
   b. If the wife had not been lovable, that she would change into a lovable wife.

c. A divorce from the husband who will not love his wife.

5. If the wife is lovable and the husband remains unloving, the major issue becomes that of how long does she remain in such a marriage. The Proverb at hand, would imply that it would not be for the rest of her life.

6. This is one more example of why we must become skillful in the art of wrestling with wisdom.

Applications Advised

1. Married men and women should be involved in Christian fellowship to a degree that they can count on their peers for help, if trouble comes to their marriage.

2. A wife who believes that her husband does not love her should work first with him, to solve the issue.

3. If that does not work, and if the wife still believes that her husband does not love her, she should check her perceptions with trusted Christian friends.

3. She should also check as to whether they think she is a lovable person, to her husband.

4. If she is judged lovable and he does not love her, then a timeline should be established for prolonged prayer….

5. If the prolonged prayer does not solve the problem, then she should decide about martyrdom. Is God offering

the gift of martyrdom to her? Does she desire this gift? Do her close companions believe that she could handle this gift? If the answer is yes to all three questions, then she should stay in the marriage until God acts....

6. If the answer is no to any question above, then set up a timeline for divorce; a timeline that matches the need for planning within the remaining strength that she has.

7. Believe that a lovable wife, who is unloved for too long a period of time, has the responsibility to initiate a divorce ...as part of God's plan for His earthly creation.

Chapter Closing Cautions

1. Persons struggling with the issues of divorce and remarriage, should be careful of their choice of church and fellowship. Choosing a lukewarm fellowship will likely yield lukewarm results, but deeply Spiritual partners will likely suggest strongly Spiritual solutions.

2. The Bill Gothard model also comes to mind in this regard, especially as we wrestle with wisdom. His method of "claiming the Hosea vision" has worked for thousands of marriages that were in trouble. On the other hand, this writer has seen first hand more than one case where Gothard's model failed. Gothard's Institute in Basic Youth Conflicts has helped millions of Christians. Sometimes, however, he too has been viewed as legalistic.

3. One especially noticeable weakness in the Gothard model is about the era in which Hosea lived. Women

were not generally able to accomplish a divorce; they were just victims of it. They were sometimes "put away" without a bill of divorcement for any number of reasons, some appropriate and some not.

Such a "put away" woman would have been used to marital privileges, and probably would not choose to go without these joys for too long a period of time. She was likely to find an adulterous relationship. This meant the risk of being stoned to death, if caught.

The risk of being stoned to death is not with us today, in America. Therefore one giant reason for Hosea's wife to go back to him, is completely missing for us. And so, the "Hosea Vision" has at least this one fatal flaw.

4. To push the "Hosea Vision" beyond its limitations, is to risk the ruination of another person's faith. Many troubled spouses have been told to just keep "praying and claiming." Sadly, they are often told by folks who are happily married and do not have a deep understanding of the issues. When years and years of prayer do not work, the separated ("put away") victim's faith may crumble.

On those occasions when the Hosea model does work, it may succeed simply because the troubled spouse is doing serious prayer for the first time in his or her life.

5. The Hosea vision may be used to force the gift of martyrdom onto someone whom God has not chosen. Well intending church leaders should be wary of the wide and simplistic use of the Hosea vision. Their failure to wrestle with wisdom about Hosea may do more harm than good.

-6-

Priceless Promises

Many Christians have used promises from the Bible for much of their lives. The promises commonly come on little cards, in a hollowed out rock, or in a plastic box with a lid to prevent loss. The Bible does contain thousands of promises, depending on who is doing the counting. Our next stop in surveying the Scriptures for divorces involves an unusual, triple promise. There are many things in this promise but our focus will be on the one related to divorce and remarriage. This "triple" promise is so unusual that most folks miss it entirely, even continually. "Triple," as used here, is in regard to being in Matthew, Mark, and Luke.

Incredible as it may seem, this "triple" promise is found in the exact same verses of three different gospels. The chapter numbers change but the verse numbers are the same. Yes, man assigned the numbers for the chapters and verses but God was watching, and helping. It is my opinion that He purposely oversaw the arranging of this rare similarity, for there are few like it. It reminds me somewhat of the "3:16" list: John 3:16, 1st Corinthians 3:16, Colossians 3:16, 2nd Timothy 3:16, etc. It is even more interesting because this triple promise is in red letters, i.e. the very words of Jesus. This matter is being strung out a bit so that it may be more memorable—for whatever future use the reader might have.

Verses *29 and 30* of Matthew 19, verses *29 and 30* of Mark 10, and verses *29 and 30* of Luke 18 comprise this triple promise as given by Jesus Himself. Each listing of this priceless promise is now given, in the King James Version as well as the New International Version (with emphasis supplied, by underlining). Please note also that triple asterisks are supplied with the word "wife" whenever the word wife has been "added," (by the KJV). More is to be said about this, under *Principles Perceived.*

1-a. KJV, Matthew 19
29 And every one that hath forsaken houses, or brethren, or sisters, or father, or mother, or ***wife, or children, or lands, for my name's sake, shall receive a hundredfold, and shall inherit everlasting life. 30 But many that are first shall be last; and the last shall be first.

1-b. NIV, Matthew 19
29 And everyone who has left houses or brothers or sisters or father or mother or children or fields for my sake will receive a hundred times as much and will

inherit eternal life. 30 But many who are first will be last, and many who are last will be first.

2-a. KJV, Mark 10

29 And Jesus answered and said, Verily I say unto you, There is no man that hath left house, or brethren, or sisters, or father, or mother, or ***wife, or children, or lands, for my sake, and the gospel's, 30 But he shall receive an hundredfold now in this time, houses, and brethren, and sisters, and mothers, and children, and lands, with persecutions; and in the world to come eternal life.

2-b. NIV, Mark 10

29 "I tell you the truth," Jesus replied, "no one who has left home or brothers or sisters or mother or father or children or fields for me and the gospel 30 will fail to receive a hundred times as much in this present age (homes, brothers, sisters, mothers, children and fields-and with them, persecutions) and in the age to come, eternal life.

3-a. KJV, Luke 18

29 And he said unto them, Verily I say unto you, There is no man that hath left house, or parents, or brethren, or wife, or children, for the kingdom of God's sake, 30 Who shall not receive manifold more in this present time, and in the world to come life everlasting.

3-b. NIV, Luke 18

29 "I tell you the truth," Jesus said to them, "no one who has left home or wife or brothers or parents or children for the sake of the kingdom of God 30 will fail to receive

many times as much in this age and, in the age to come, eternal life."

Principles Perceived

1. In the half dozen listings above, the reward of a hundred times as much is a constant promise. Luke varies by stating: manifold more or many times as much. One might also call the promise priceless. The description of one hundred times as much would certainly be "priceless" in terms of houses or fields....

2. The KJV has "added" the word wife, in Matthew and Mark. It is worth noting here that the KJV "adds" hundreds of words that were not there in the original Greek manuscripts. So this addition of the word "wife" is not suspicious in regard to any special agenda.

3. Luke gives the word wife in both the KJV and NIV. Perhaps most importantly, wife is stated in the Greek, in the gospel of Luke. Interestingly, husband is not listed in the Greek, the KJV, the NIV, or any other Bible known to this writer.

4. The addition of the word wife by the KJV in both Matthew and Mark was apparently for two reasons: a. the context, and b. the Greek manuscripts—some of them say wife and some do not. Since Luke manuscripts are strong with the word wife, the KJV apparently opted for synoptic uniformity.

5. The weight of the evidence here would say that the KJV has a "more telling" translation than the NIV in regard to the use of the word wife.

6. Other important issues are within these verses but this list of principles is reduced in order to keep the focus of this promise on *"Divorce as 'Required' by Scripture."*

7. The promise can have fulfillment in a figurative sense, a literal sense, or both.

8. Obtaining the promised reward hinges on at least these two things:

   a. giving up what is usually quite valuable, and

   b. giving up valuable (for the invaluable) for Jesus' sake, i.e. for the sake of the Kingdom of God.

9. Giving up family for the Kingdom could include:

   a. what the apostles James and John did when they dropped their nets, left their father Zebedee, and followed Jesus (Mt 4:21-22).

   b. the follower of Jesus, who was told by Jesus to, "let the dead bury their own dead (Mt 8:22). This disciple faced the need to bury his own dad but was told by Jesus to let somebody else do it. The Kingdom was more important!

c. what Jesus did when He left His Father in Heaven, to come down to earth as the sin sacrifice for all who would come to believe in Him.

d. an example similar to that of Ezekiel as found in Ezek. 24:15-18. The word of the LORD came to me: 16 "Son of man, with one blow I am about to take away from you the delight of your eyes. Yet do not lament or weep or shed any tears. 17 Groan quietly; do not mourn for the dead. Keep your turban fastened and your sandals on your feet; do not cover the lower part of your face or eat the customary food [of mourners]." 18 So I spoke to the people in the morning, and in the evening my wife died. The next morning I did as I had been commanded. NIV (underline supplied). What kind of a man would not mourn for a wife who had been the "delight of his eyes?"

e. the issue of hate as told by Jesus in Luke 14:26, "If anyone comes to me and does not hate his father and mother, his wife and children, his brothers and sisters-yes, even his own life-he cannot be my disciple." (underlining supplied). The NIV (above) and many other good translations use the word hate, as does the original Greek. It is a strong word. Jesus may have been exaggerating for impact, but maybe he meant exactly what he said. There are other related verses, and commentators, who say that Jesus simply meant that a follower of His must love Him more. Such love may be seen as "hate" turned inside out.

f. a drug addict who gives up his rebellious ways to follow Christ, and goes into Christian rehab, at a place far from his "loving" but un-Christian family.

g. a Christian husband who finally "gives up" on his un-Christian wife when she sues him for divorce. He simply signs the papers or refuses to fight in court, to "save" his marriage.

10. The Christian husband, just mentioned above, should be able to expect a reward. Opponents to this idea might think that such a man would not be rewarded due to a hundred wives being polygamy—against the will of God. On the other hand, supporters to this thinking might easily come to the conclusion that the divorced man would receive from God a one-hundred-fold wife.

If the other "give ups" for the Kingdom yield a hundred fold increase, why wouldn't a "given-up-wife" yield a one-hundred-fold wife? The homes and fields are to be received in this life—here on earth. Surely the wife issue would also be handled while the husband is still here on earth.

The manner in which this matter occurs in New Testament times is to be discussed in the next chapter, '*Dutiful Divorces.*' For now let's get on to applications and cautions.

Applications Advised

1. A husband who would give up his un-Christian wife for the sake of the Kingdom of God should "normally"

expect the Lord to reward him with a one-hundred-fold wife.

2. "Abnormal" should also be addressed just now. A minority of divorced men should never remarry. Paul recommended celibacy, and had probably once been married. On the other hand, all of the original apostles had wives, as noted in 1st Corinthians 9:5. They seemed to be the "norm." Therefore, the "abnormal" would be to remain celibate. Hear also Jesus' directive on this issue in Matthew 19:12:

> "For some are eunuchs because they were born that way; others were made that way by men; and others have renounced marriage because of the kingdom of heaven. The one who can accept this should accept it." NIV, with underlining supplied.

3. Due to the probability of being in the Last Days, church folks should expect some "extreme" measures such as those applied to Ezekiel by God. We do not expect such violence as was normal in the Old Testament—the death of Ezekiel's wife. On the other hand, we should expect God's "extreme" intervention in any number of marriages that have been displeasing to Him for too long a period of time. Some of His servants are suffering in so many ways, and in so many places. They need Him to rescue them—especially in their homes!

3-A. NOTE: Jerusalem was overrun by the Gentiles for about 2500 years—until that stopped in 1967. The Gentiles have been in their very last days ever since. The return of Israel to her homeland is an undeniable sign that

God is getting ready to again put the Jew ahead of the Gentile. Daily news also shows that we live in that desperate, end-of-days generation. Such desperate times will likely call for some "desperate" measures.

4. Bible promises should be accepted, regardless of whether we agree with their outcome. Helpful "tradition" must be set aside when the word of God is making exceptions to it. A one-hundred-fold wife should be upheld—to be just as Biblical as "you reap what you sow." The same should be true for a one-hundred-fold husband.

Chapter Closing Cautions

1. This writer has gotten rather close to "worst case analysis" in this chapter. Some may say that this whole chapter is based on such logic. They are requested to study the heavy-duty language used by Jesus, and then reconsider the data in this chapter.

2. Remember also Jesus' words about "persecutions," as found in Mark's version of the priceless promise. Folks who are "sold-out" for the Kingdom of God will receive priceless rewards but they are also going to receive their share of sufferings.

3. Lukewarm or backslidden Christians should not even dream about the priceless promise—unless they are also decided to seek Him with their whole heart, once and for all. (References for study in this regard include John 14:21, and Jeremiah 29:13.)

4. The "priceless promise" in this chapter carries a high price tag—but that high payment is still a great bargain!

5. If any number of Jesus' followers is to receive this priceless promise, then a similar number of them will face a divorce "required" by Scripture. Omitting this truth takes away from the words of God, and that is dangerous.

-7-

Dutiful Divorces

Let go—and let God! Have you seen that bumper sticker? Perhaps you have seen this quip on a balloon. It has been popular in the US for many years. It fairly well summarizes the bottom line for this chapter.

That saying has been rather helpful for Christians who are worriers. Philippians 4:6 advises us not to be anxious about anything; however, not that many of us have memorized that verse. So the balloon and bumper sticker can be very helpful.

Some Christians believe that this little saying is irresponsible. In some cases, they may be correct. One problem related to worry, or concern, is that "letting go" of a spouse is usually and immediately seen as a sin. My purpose in writing this chapter is to convince the reader that the opposite is true. That is to say—that sometimes the failure to "let go" of a spouse may be what amounts to sin. This may be the "toughest sell" of this whole book. Is it a Christian duty to "let go," or not? 1st Corinthians 7:12-16 (underlining supplied) states:

New International Version -- 12 To the rest I say this (I, not the Lord): If any brother has a wife who is not a believer and she is willing to live with him, he must not divorce her. 13 And if a woman has a husband who is not a believer and he is willing to live with her, she must not divorce him. 14 For the unbelieving husband has been sanctified through his wife, and the unbelieving wife has been sanctified through her believing husband. Otherwise your children would be unclean, but as it is, they are holy. 15 But if the unbeliever leaves, let him do so. A believing man or woman is not bound in such circumstances; God has called us to live in peace. 16 How do you know, wife, whether you will save your husband? Or, how do you know, husband, whether you will save your wife?

King James Version -- 12 But to the rest speak I, not the Lord: If any brother hath a wife that believeth not, and she be pleased to dwell with him, let him not put her away. 13 And the woman which hath an husband that believeth not, and if he be pleased to dwell with her, let her not leave him. 14 For the unbelieving husband is sanctified by the wife, and the unbelieving wife is sanctified by the husband: else were your children unclean; but now are they holy. 15 But if the unbelieving depart, let him depart. A brother or a sister is not under bondage in such cases: but God hath called us to peace.

16 For what knowest thou, O wife, whether thou shalt save thy husband? or how knowest thou, O man, whether thou shalt save thy wife?

It all seems so clear when focusing on the underlines. The problem comes when other issues are faced. One of those other issues is how to decide who is a believer and who is not.

The church has several impediments today in regard to saying *who* is a believer. Several of the reasons for this should probably be listed before getting into our usual principles, applications and cautions. Many could be given but here is a partial list of those impediments:

> 1st Impediment - Lukewarmness. Hot water is easy to detect; cold is also. But Jesus spoke against the lukewarm (in Revelation 3:15-16). He said that he would vomit them out of His body (the church). Apparently most of the Laodicean Church was lukewarm. They were in His body—but might as well not have been. The same is often true today. If you are in a lukewarm church, your faith is not likely to be worth much. You may not even be able to tell if you are a Christian.

> 2nd Impediment - Assimilation. Many churches today favor the model of assimilation. They invite people to be part of their worship hour and Sunday School—but wait sometimes for a year or more to speak about the need to be born again. During this time many other folks in that "fellowship" do not

know who is a Christian and who is not. Church leaders also are not sure about who is a Christian.

Contrast this to the church model found in Acts 5, where even the unbelievers knew who the believers were! NIV verses 12-14 read:

12 The apostles performed many miraculous signs and wonders among the people. And all the believers used to meet together in Solomon's Colonnade. 13 No one else dared join them, even though they were highly regarded by the people. 14 Nevertheless, more and more men and women believed in the Lord and were added to their number. (Underlining supplied.)

Apparently there was some anointing, or power, or obvious change of lifestyle that marked a believer. How about your church? Can you say for sure who is a believer and who is not?

3rd Impediment -- Spiritual gifts missing. Discernment is one of the Spiritual gifts. It would normally be thought of as rather helpful with deciding who has the Spirit of Jesus and who has embraced other spirits. How many leaders in today's churches can say that they definitely have the gift of discernment? Wisdom is also a Spiritual gift. Without this gift, many lukewarms get by with appearing to be good Christians. They could do much more for the Lord but nobody notices because nobody has the wisdom to know their true capabilities.

4th Impediment -- Fear. In the first half of the last century, "fruit inspecting" became popular in the church. This practice was good but as usual it went too far. In the second half of the last century, "fruit inspecting" was perceived as bad, and was generally abandoned. Many of today's leaders are fearful of being seen as "fruit inspectors." They therefore stay too far away from decision making in regard to who is, and who is not, a believer.

One extra-special fear is about suggesting the break up of a bad marriage after finding one party to be a believer and the other one not.

5th Impediment - Dynamics. Life moves forward at one pace or another until death. Personality and character are therefore in need of continual development. This is especially true of Christian character. In Jesus' time, to be considered as one of His believers, a person would follow after Him in every way possible. A new believer today can keep his current Christian character in a static condition. However, as his or her life "grows," such a static condition will likely result in automatic backsliding. Life is dynamic and being like Jesus requires dynamic practices and disciplines that put Jesus first. Without this constant "push" by all concerned, believers can easily lose their first love and not even care that much about it. (See Revelation 2:4-5.)

All of these impediments make it almost impossible in many cases for the church, or an individual believer, to decide about the case of the unbelieving spouse. The end result is that most folks are told to try and stick it out, in hopes of saving a marriage. This advice in many cases is directly against the "let go" of 1st Corinthians 7:15. As stated previously, there are any number of times when allowing a divorce is dutiful in light of that verse.

Doesn't it feel better to have the scales of Scripture weighing "re-centered" by 1st Corinthians 7:15? We should now be ready for principles, applications, and cautions—about verses 12 thru 15, given again below:

New International Version -- 12 To the rest I say this (I, not the Lord): If any brother has a wife who is not a believer and she is willing to live with him, he must not divorce her. 13 And if a woman has a husband who is not a believer and he is willing to live with her, she must not divorce him. 14 For the unbelieving husband has been sanctified through his wife, and the unbelieving wife has been sanctified through her believing husband. Otherwise your children would be unclean, but as it is, they are holy. 15 But if the unbeliever leaves, let him do so. A believing man or woman is not bound in such circumstances; God has called us to live in peace. 16 How do you know, wife, whether you will save your husband? Or, how do you know, husband, whether you will save your wife?

Principles Perceived

1. A believing spouse has a duty to allow an unbelieving spouse to leave. In today's society, that will usually mean

a divorce "required" by Scripture. One related question is who may, or must, initiate this divorce. Normally it would be the unbeliever. However, there may be instances where the believer would have to initiate the divorce, for any number of reasons. One example would be abandonment.

2. The phrase "willing to live with," in verse 12, appears to carry a lot of weight. What might it mean? Verse 15 offers contextual help; it talks about living in peace. Any issue which breaks that peace for too long a period of time amounts to an unwillingness "to live with" the other spouse. As you probably already know, there are so very many ways for the unbeliever (or the believer) "to leave" the marriage. It is not just a physical move out of the house or apartment.

3. Deciding with certainty about who is unwilling to live with the other can be an impossible task. Do we yet know with certainty whether O.J. Simpson murdered his wife? Murder involves a huge issue of unwillingness. Lesser issues are often much more difficult to measure with certainty. Remember that one part of '*Serious Safeguards.*' That is: nothing can be firmly established except on the strength of two or more witnesses....

4. The judgment about which spouse is unwilling to live with the other will often have to be left with the two spouses. Only supernatural, Spiritual discernment will otherwise be enough to make such judgments. In the absence of the supernatural, outsiders must wait on the Lord—until two witnesses are available. This may never

occur. Until it does occur, outsiders should simply love and support wounded spouses as much as their resources allow, and as led by the Spirit.

5. Believers who have been divorced are no longer "bound." Here too is a can of worms. Many highly respected Christian leaders are on opposite sides in regard to what it means to no longer be "bound." Some say remarriage is obviously okay; others say no such thing can be presumed.

This writer has concluded from other portions of Scripture that remarriage, or no remarriage, are both okay with the good Lord. It does not have to be one or the other.

Consider again Jesus' teaching about eunuchs. Those who can accept, or achieve, the gift of celibacy are encouraged to do so. However those without the gift should not be forced into it. Again, the original apostles had wives, and Paul did not. These were the highest and most authoritative followers of Jesus in the first century. They modeled marriage and celibacy, but the ratio was eleven to one in favor of marriage.

In Genesis 2:18, God said that it was not good for man to live alone. In 1st Corinthians 7:2, Paul wrote that each man should have a wife and each woman a husband. In 7:7, Paul wished that all men were single (as he was), but he acknowledged that one (man) has this gift (celibacy), and another man has another gift (marriage).

For the record this writer finds God ordained martyrdom to be the highest of all unlisted gifts; and celibacy to be the second highest, and unlisted, gift. These "unlisted" gifts are in a class of their own. They may actually exceed the top-listed gift (or office), i.e. the rank of apostle. See 1st Corinthians 12:28. Of course, love is the greatest gift—but it is a general gift.

The bottom line on "not bound" is that the believer (or the unbeliever) may remarry if he or she chooses to do so. 1st Corinthians 7:32-35 makes great observations on the choice. The expected ratio of celibacy "versus" remarriage is at least 11 to 1 in favor of remarriage. By the way, this means that most of those divorced men at the end of Ezra did remarry. Nothing is new under the sun; what has been will be, and what is has already been. (See Ecclesiastes 1:9; 3:15.)

6. In a truly peaceful marriage between a believer and an unbeliever, the believer would have primary responsibility, and authority, to make moral judgments. Otherwise the children might follow the unbeliever and become unclean.

7. A mixed marriage can produce a holy home. Notice in verse 14 that the unbeliever is sanctified by the believer and that the children are holy—if the unbeliever is willing to "live with" the believer. This is directly related to the preceding number 6.

8. A believing spouse has no guarantee of saving his or her unbelieving spouse.

9. It appears that Paul sometimes got information directly from the Lord Jesus and that sometimes he got it from the (Holy) Spirit. See verses 10, 12, & 40, of 1st Corinthians chapter 7.

Applications Advised

1. Accept divorce as one of the duties of a Christian, whenever the unbelieving spouse has left the marriage. Be ready to explain this "duty" to a Christian who is in need and unaware of it.

2. Avoid the use of this common phrase, "the sin of divorce." Do not support those who apply it broadly to both spouses of a divorce. Pray for those users of this phrase—that they might understand the injury produced by their unwise word choice. Pray for the church at large to understand that one spouse (or both) may sin during divorce but that a believing spouse is often not in any sin during divorce.

3. If you are a believer, and are married to an unbeliever, be careful not to take unfair advantage of the divorce duty described in this chapter. Do not "drive" the unbeliever out. He or she may leave but you will need a clear conscience before God that you did not drive him or her out.

4. All parties involved with, or concerned about, divorcing (or separated) spouses must be careful not to take sides unless (and until) two or more witnesses have helped establish enough truth about the whole situation. Even if good witnesses have established undeniable truth in one area of concern, remember to put this information into the perspective of the whole marriage. Do not let the squeaking wheel get all the grease. Examine the other wheels too.

5. Believers (and unbelievers) who divorce should expect plenty of suffering at the hands of those who have no room for any divorce.

6. If you are a believer, and are married to an unbeliever, who lives peaceably with you, do not worry about your children. Be a sanctifying force in your marriage and have faith that the children will be holy.

7. If you are the believing wife of an unbelieving husband, do not worry about breaking the headship doctrine of 1st Corinthians 11:3. Remember how Shiphrah & Puah "broke the rules" to save lives and God rewarded them (Exodus ch. 1). God makes the rules. He also allows them to be broken for a higher good. You must make the moral and Spiritual choices in your marriage, as led by the Bible and the Holy Spirit—in order to raise good children. It is worth noting here that most other headship issues could, and perhaps should, be left for your husband to make.

8. Do not listen to those denominations that say the men at the end of Ezra stayed single for the rest of their lives. Do not believe their argument, about the absence of verses reporting remarriage by these men, as proof that they never remarried. Absence of such discussion neither proves nor disproves remarriage. On the other hand, Bible harmony would lean strongly toward their remarriage. Believe that celibacy is actually a rare gift, as proven by The Eleven Apostles & Paul. Consider also these related verses from 1st Timothy:

> 4:1 The Spirit clearly says that in later times some will abandon the faith and follow deceiving spirits and things taught by demons. 2 Such teachings come through hypocritical liars, whose consciences have been seared as with a hot iron. 3 They forbid people to marry.... (NIV, underlining supplied)

9. Do not hold onto a marriage solely for the sake of saving your unsaved spouse. Our verses (earlier) state that there is no guarantee of this occurring. Actually, in some cases, the letting go might be more helpful to the unsaved partner. Consider how God let go of Israel, for her own good, in Jeremiah 3:8, as underlined below:

> 6 During the reign of King Josiah, the LORD said to me, "Have you seen what faithless Israel has done? She has gone up on every high hill and under every spreading tree and has committed adultery there. 7 I thought that after she had done all this she would return to me but she did not, and her unfaithful sister Judah saw it. 8 I gave faithless Israel her certificate of divorce and sent her away because of all her adulteries. (NIV)

If it is true that God hates divorce, *then why* did He do it? If divorce is sinful, did He sin? Obviously not! Isaiah 50:1 also records the certificate of divorce given by God to Israel. The Hebrew word used here is "keriythuwth." Note also that the context for "adulteries" in these verses is primarily about idols. Jeremiah was being figurative. The Israelites had bowed down to many false idols on many high hills....

10. Believe that sometimes, under dire circumstances, to be like God is to get divorced—at least for a while. God divorced Israel (see above).

Prophecy experts use Hosea 6:2 to show that God is finally about to take Israel back. However God lives forever and we do not. Israel-the-divorcee' can look forward to remarriage with Him. On the other hand, most divorced humans should simply remarry.

11. Christians who remarry must remarry to a Christian. If they knowingly yoke with an unbeliever, they sin (2nd Corinthians 6:14).

Chapter Closing Cautions

1. Too much freedom "in the Lord" can easily become a license to sin. Being openly submissive to a good cell (or care) group should prevent such license.

2. Martyrdom that is "sought" can easily turn into a martyr complex. This can lead to serious mental health issues, and should otherwise be avoided due to poor health influences in general.

3. Some unbelievers appear, on the surface, to be living peaceably with their believing spouse. However, when questions arise about passive-aggressive characteristics, manipulation, projection, anger, and other such serious misbehavior—professional counseling is likely to needed. This is especially true when the believer is not as mentally sharp, or aggressive, as the unbeliever is.

4. Christians who stay married to unbelievers can become guilty of "spiritual" co-dependency, in those cases where the unbeliever is deterred from leaving.

5. Any believer who directly, or subtly, drives out an unbelieving spouse may expect to be disciplined by God. The level of unfairness, on the part of the believer, may be returned to the believer by God. Even accidental pushing away of the unbeliever is not likely to be overlooked by God. Believers have a serious responsibility to set a good example of how a Christian spouse loves his or her mate.

7. Born again believers are new creations; the old has gone and the new has come (2nd Corinthians 5:17). Failure to use this standard, when appropriate, is to lose one large piece of the wisdom of Scripture—in regard to issues of divorce and remarriage.

8. Christians should not decrease the importance of what Paul said in 1st Corinthians 7:12 (and following) just because he said "(I, not the Lord)." Later, in verse 40 (NIV), he said, "...and I think that I too have the Spirit of God." And all Scripture is God-breathed (2nd Tim 3:16).

In the same way, 1st Corinthians 7:10-11 is not more Scriptural just because Paul said, "(not I, but the Lord)." It probably just means that the Lord Jesus Christ gave this part directly to the apostle Paul, and he is telling us about that directness.

-8-

Timothy, Titus & Taboo

In the church, divorce is a common taboo for a bishop, an elder, an overseer, a pastor, a Sunday School superintendent, a teacher, etc. Have you heard of this taboo? Or, is it just part of the "hidden agenda" in your church? This writer believes that divorce should be far from normal for church leaders, but to make it taboo, is to go beyond what Timothy and Titus state.

Remarriage for a church leader is more than a common taboo; it is often a total taboo. This chapter explores the shaky foundation for that blanket taboo. Required divorces will also be found in this chapter.

Short texts help give this chapter a narrow focus. The short texts at issue come from 1st Timothy 3:2 and Titus 1:6. Here they are, with underlining supplied, in the

King James Version (KJV), New International Version (NIV), and NIV-with one correction back to the original Greek:

KJV, 1st Timothy 3: - 2 A bishop then must be blameless, the husband of one wife, vigilant, sober, of good behaviour, given to hospitality, apt to teach;

NIV, 1st Timothy 3: - 2 Now the overseer must be above reproach, the husband of but one wife, temperate, self-controlled, respectable, hospitable, able to teach,

NIV "corrected," 1st Timothy 3: - 2 Now the overseer must be above reproach, the husband of ~~but~~ one wife, temperate, self-controlled, respectable, hospitable, able to teach,

---

KJV, Titus 1: - 6 If any be blameless, the husband of one wife, having faithful children not accused of riot or unruly.

NIV, Titus 1: - 6 An elder must be blameless, the husband of but one wife, a man whose children believe and are not open to the charge of being wild and disobedient.

NIV "corrected," Titus 1: - 6 An elder must be blameless, the husband of ~~but~~ one wife, a man whose children believe and are not open to the charge of being wild and disobedient.

Principles Perceived

1. NOTE: To help avoid repetition of terms, the word "overseer" will usually be applied as the equivalent for the variety of church leaders who have authority over other Christians.

2. Overseers must be men (they are husbands of wives).

3. Overseers must currently be husbands.

4. Overseers must be husbands of only one wife.

5. The NIV adds the word "but." This tiny addition makes a huge change in the meaning of the requirement in focus.

6. The issue of only ever having one wife is open to much debate—as the next several points will show.

7. Further investigation shows the tiny word "but" to be at the crux of a centuries long debate. That information is given now to help "settle" the case, for the upcoming applications.

8. There are many respected scholars on both sides of the issue: "married" versus "married-only-once," for eligibility as overseer. Here are a half dozen sources on one side and a half dozen on the other side.

   a. married: John Chrysostom, John Calvin, Adam

Clarke, *Barne's Notes, Robertson's New Testament Word Pictures,* and *Vine's Expository Dictionary of New Testament Words*

b. married-only-once: Gleason Archer, Matthew Henry, Kenneth Wuest, *Jamieson, Fausset & Brown Commentary, Jerome Biblical Commentary, Vincent's New Testament Word Studies*

c. It is worth noting that some of these sources seem quite sure of themselves, while others openly admit their inability to say for sure.

9. The focus point for interpretation seems to be the word "one," i.e. "mias" (mia) in the Greek (Strong's 3391). It can mean one—as in one, two, three.... Or, it can mean one—as in first, or chief. In this latter use, it would mean one wife and only one. In the former case, it would mean one wife as of the present time.

10. Paul used this word "mias" for each of the three times he wrote about the husband of one wife in Timothy & Titus. Paul also used this word in many other places; several examples follow:

a. the one flesh of 1st Corinthians 6:16
b. that one day of 1st Corinthians 10:8
c. the minus one lash of 2nd Corinthians 11:24
d. the one faith of Ephesians 4:5
e. the one man (or mind) of Philippians 1:27

11. A look at Paul's many uses of "mias" does not narrow its meaning to one as in one, two, three; or one as in first,

or chief. Even the contexts do not firmly pin it down. It is easy to see why so many godly men disagree on which way to go with the word "one." Let's leave the Greek and go to the commentators.

12. Among the commentators' arguments is the issue of polygamy. Apparently, it was widely practiced among the gentiles, and sometimes by the Jews. To become an overseer, one would have to give up, or "let go" of any extra wives. This much seems certain on the part of most scholars. It will also (finally) lead to the main reason for writing this chapter -when *Applications* are addressed.

13. Observe also that Timothy and Titus are being prescriptive. That is, they are listing normal qualities for an overseer. Actual descriptions of appointed overseers probably did not measure up to such perfectionism. One huge proof of this is Paul. He was not then the current husband of one wife. He probably was once married but was no longer married (for whatever reason). How then could Paul be an overseer of overseers? One answer is that the listings in Timothy and Titus are prescriptive, and that grace would occasionally have to cover one or more inadequacies among those listings of qualifications for an overseer.

Grace is mentioned on behalf of Paul (above). This does not mean that he was in sin, and needed grace to cover it. It does mean that the letter of the law kills, and that the Spirit gives life. For example, under the "law," if Paul was single, how could he have his household under control (as required by Timothy & Titus)? However, under "grace," we can easily see that he had a number of children who were under control, e.g. Timothy—his son in the faith.

Applications Advised

1. Have a worldview when applying the Scriptures. All through history, polygamy has been a problem. This means, at a minimum, and perhaps primarily, that the husband of one wife was aimed at polygamists (and/or bigamists).

2. Men who are polygamists when they are saved, will have to reduce themselves to one wife if they want to quality as an overseer.

3. Believe, if you can, that #2 (immediately above), is a worthy reason for an entire chapter like this one.

4. Believe that #2 above is one more proof for *"Divorce as 'Required 'by Scripture."* As we have seen before, (e.g. Exodus 21), the word "divorce" is not used in Timothy or Titus. However, the fulfillment of the qualifications for overseer will, in many foreign (& polygamous) cultures, require divorce....

5. Admire the apparent intent of the NIV when it states the "husband of but one wife" but lean more toward the original Greek "husband of one wife." Neither the Greek nor many good scholars can prove the need to add that word "but."

6. My admiration for the NIV wording includes the context of the overseer being above reproach (blameless). It would be great if all overseers had only one wife for their whole life.

7. On the other hand, one must also look at the context of an entire life. For example, Paul persecuted Christians unto death. He stood by approvingly while Stephen was stoned. Yet God chose Paul to be the "greatest" apostle.

8. Readers should believe that overseer qualifications are not to be applied legalistically. The idea of being the husband of one wife (or of but one) was being broken by Paul even as he wrote it. He was a single man.

9. If we accept Paul as an overseer of overseers, then we cannot reject a man who is divorced & remarried—on the simple basis of not having had "but" one wife. Such a taboo is hypocrisy. Such a taboo against an "innocently" divorced man is worse than hypocrisy. Such a taboo makes divorce & remarriage worse than murder (or conspiring to do many murders). This too is silly.

Chapter Closing Cautions

1. All writers risk being subjective. That is, they may let their personal wishes influence their writing. The writer of this book is no exception.

2. My efforts to prevent subjectivity include openness. It would have been easier for me to omit this chapter. It is not one of the strongest supports for the theme of this

book. Openness meant writing it anyway (and including it in this book).

3. Please weigh the propositions put forward in this chapter (and this book) for yourself. Does the evidence offered make good sense? Are the sources credible? Do you have any witness in your spirit that this book is not only well intended, but also within Scriptural patterns?

4. When any particular Bible passage yields more than one interpretation, it will usually need a lot more work than those that are simple.

5. A broadminded way to handle "husband of one wife" versus "husband of but one wife" is to treat it like predestination. Millions of Christians have believed that God predestines human beings to Heaven or Hell. Even more millions believe that He would never do such a thing. Both "camps" have been used by the Lord to do His will. Therefore, predestination must not be a hugely important thing to God. But what if one "camp" (or the other) were to be put into the non-useable category of "taboo?" What would God think of that?

-9-

Applying "Apoluo"

Theory is one thing but practice is another. In the chapter entitled *'Converted by Callison,'* a good amount of material was given about "apoluo" versus "apostasion." A fair amount of that material was theoretical. It now seems to be time for getting down to cases....

In this chapter, the survey about divorces centers on those verses so often used to forbid divorce (and remarriage). This chapter is believed to be necessary in order to further prove the errors of those who forbid divorce and remarriage. They are not being held up for any personal ridicule. One problem is that their reliance on modern translations has let them down.

This chapter has been held back until most of the other "groundwork" could be laid. My hope is that the reader will now have a fairly open mind for the cases presented here. Some readers may find that these cases belabor the issues at hand. These readers are welcome to skip, or just skim, this chapter. Their primary loss would be further proofs of how the King James Version did better on this one word "apoluo" than did the NIV (and other modern translations). Other readers are likely to need, or want, these additional proofs. Such reading also adds much to the case for *converting* to Callison.

The organization of these "cases" involves quoting Jesus in the eleven areas where He "applied" the word "apoluo." Some other applications of apoluo will also be given, e.g. Joseph had in mind to "put Mary away," and believers' separation (1st Corinthians 7:10-11). Case, as used here, refers to any occurrence of the word apoluo. If it occurs twice in a verse, that is two cases. Cases are numbered inside of [brackets]. Each "application" quotes from: (1) the King James Version, (2) *The New Testament: An Expanded Translation,* (3) the New International Version, and (4) the NIV with a correction. This correction usually means one slight but important change, i.e. changing the word divorce to the words "put away."

Until now the term "put away" has been highlighted with quotation marks. Capitalization will now be used instead, as its usage by Jesus is traced through the KJV. Commentary will then be given about how much better sense the NIV, or any other modern translation, would make if the term "put away" were used. Underlining will be supplied as needed, without notation in the cases.

Special credit should be noted here for number (2) above: *The New Testament: An Expanded Translation* by Kenneth S. Wuest. As reported by Walter Callison, this "modern" translation always applies "put away" when apoluo is in the original Greek. The Wuest translation, "uses as many English words as are necessary to bring out the full richness, force, and clarity of the original text." It is not a paraphrase, or an interpretation—but a unique translation. The Wuest New Testament was reprinted in 2002 (ISBN # 0-8028-0882-4), and is available in paperback.

Kenneth Wuest himself also deserves special recognition, especially for those who might not have heard of him. At his death in 1962, he was "Teacher Emeritus of New Testament Greek," at Moody Bible Institute in Chicago, Illinois. Wuest authored dozens of books—many of which were published by the prestigious Eerdmans Publishing Company. Moody Bible Institute is so well known that no introduction is needed. Surely this Greek scholar would have known how to properly apply the word "apoluo. " He consistently wrote "put away," or the equivalent word "dismiss." (Either usage by Wuest may later turn into actual divorce but neither usage, per se, includes a writ of divorcement.)

This all-important term "put away" should be discussed again. It is applied for the Greek word "apoluo" for all cases but one, in the King James Version. That one exception is an error, and should have been the same as the other occurrences. "Put away" basically means, even usually means, to separate (but not divorce).

"Put away" had in Moses' day, and still has in our time, proper and improper uses. A faithful husband may properly "put away" his wife if she is found to have venereal disease. The same is true for the faithful wife whose husband gets VD through unfaithfulness. The length of time for being "put away" is directly related to how long it takes to be cured of the disease.

Other uses for "putting away" one's spouse may not be appropriate, or helpful. Some examples include: bad manners, untidiness, overweight, unsightliness, etc.

In its cruelest form, a man would send his wife out of the home to fend for herself without any help from her husband. The husband would refuse to give her the bill of divorcement required in Deuteronomy 24. Therefore she could not find another husband (as allowed by Dt. 24). As her destitution increased and lengthened, she might turn to an adulterous relationship for which she could be stoned to death. Her husband would then have essentially murdered her without lifting a finger. This writer wonders about the woman who was caught in the act of adultery and brought before Jesus. Was she "put away" by a cruel, hardhearted man? Such "putting away" may be what God hated in Malachi 2:16. (This writer believes that it was not divorce…that He hated.)

[1st] *Case> Matthew 5:31*

KJV - 31 It hath been said, Whosoever shall [1] PUT AWAY his wife, let him give her a writing of divorcement:

Wuest - 31 Moreover, it was said, Whoever [1] dismisses his wife, let him give her a bill of divorce.

NIV - 31 "It has been said, 'Anyone who [1] divorces his wife must give her a certificate of divorce.'

NIV corrected - "It has been said, 'Anyone who [1] ~~divorces~~ puts away his wife must give her a certificate of divorce.'

1st Case> Commentary

1. Commentator Adam Clarke offers a common form of divorcement as used in Bible times. Here is a quote from that form, with John & Jane Doe being added: "I (John Doe) with entire consent of mind, and without any compulsion, have (hereby) divorced, dismissed, and expelled (Jane Doe)." Notice the three separate actions: (a) *divorced,* (b) *dismissed,* and (c) *expelled.* These three actions could take place in a matter of days, weeks, or many months. In his heart, John would separate himself from his wife and decide to go through with the writing of a bill of divorcement. John would hand the bill of divorcement to his wife--making her dismissal official. John would verbally expel Jane by telling her to leave....

2. This combination of actions met the requirements of the Law of Moses, in Deuteronomy 24:1-3.

3. The NIV is obviously overlapping itself when it states, 'Anyone who divorces his wife must give her a certificate of divorce.' How can someone divorce his wife without a

certificate of divorce? Why tell someone to do what has to be part of the action being taken? It would be like saying anyone who throws a snowball must have a snowball (to throw). The NIV translation does not make very good sense. The other two translations do make good sense, as does the corrected NIV.

4. According to Moses, a husband who was ending his relationship with his wife had to do more than just (a)"put away" his wife permanently, or (b) send his wife away desolately, or (c) verbally dismiss his wife from the marriage. Any one of these three phrases makes perfectly good sense in the context of Matthew 5:31.

1st Case> Impact on Divorce and Remarriage

No noteworthy issues for this 1st case.

[2nd and 3rd] *Cases> Matthew 5:32* -With introductory note: fornication is a broad term; adultery is a narrow term. Fornication is porneia in the Greek, with a Strong's number of 4202; adultery is moicheia in the Greek, with a Strong's number of 3430. Since there is some overlap of meaning, the Strong's number is given beside each of these two words–to indicate difference and definition.

KJV - 32 But I say unto you, That whosoever shall [2] PUT AWAY his wife, saving for the cause of fornication-4202, causeth her to commit adultery-3430: and whosoever shall marry her that is [3] divorced committeth adultery-3430. (The word divorced here is "apoluo" in the Greek, i.e. PUT AWAY. This case #3 is that one error by the KJV.)

Wuest - 32 But as for myself, I am saying to you, Everyone who [2] dismisses his wife except in a case of unchastity-4202, causes her to commit adultery-3430, and whoever marries her who has been [3] dismissed, commits adultery-3430.

NIV - 32 But I tell you that anyone who [2] divorces his wife, except for marital unfaithfulness-4202, causes her to become an adulteress-3430, and anyone who marries the [3] divorced woman commits adultery-3430.

NIV corrected - 32 But I tell you that anyone who [2] ~~divorces~~ puts away his wife, except for marital unfaithfulness-4202, causes her to become an adulteress-3430, and anyone who marries the [3] ~~divorced~~ put away woman commits adultery-3430.

2nd and 3rd Cases> Commentary

1. Here is the only error by the KJV; it appears at the end of verse 32. This error was corrected in the 1881 KJV and in the 1901 ASV.

2. The obviousness of this KJV error can be seen within the verse itself. It was the same woman in the first clause as it was in the second clause. Therefore the same word, or term (put away), would apply to both the early part of the sentence and the latter part. (The first clause is the first 23 words; the second clause begins with the word "and.")

3. Three terms about *immoral behavior* come into play in this case, i.e. fornication-KJV, unchastity-Wuest, and marital unfaithfulness-NIV. Other similar terms include whoredom, incest, and harlotry. Adultery can be included as one type of *immoral behavior* but it is too narrow to be a proper, or "equivalent," interpretation for any of the terms at stake in this paragraph. These terms are important to the issue of making sense of the two cases under scrutiny.

4. Perhaps "marital unfaithfulness," as suggested by the NIV, is the best interpretation for our purposes. Remember though that in the Old Testament this meant of the flesh. In the New Testament it means of the flesh, <u>or</u> just in the mind/heart (Mt 5:28).

5. Jesus was apparently saying that a husband could "put his wife away" for "marital unfaithfulness" of the flesh (or "marital unfaithfulness" of the heart) <u>and not</u> be guilty of causing her to commit adultery. In this type of case the husband did not have to give a bill of divorce. In fact that husband may not even have wanted to divorce his wife.

5-A. IMPORTANT NOTE: The word "adultery," here used by Jesus, has also just been redefined by Jesus. In the immediately preceding verses, Jesus had "raised the bar" in regard to adultery. (See Matthew 5:27-30.) Adultery now included just a lustful look.... This higher standard is important to understanding the text. A man (or woman) could now be guilty of adultery without having committed some concretely visible act.

Therefore, the wife who was caused to commit adultery...may have done so only in her mind. Her adultery could also now include figurative adultery of a broad nature, i.e. any marital unfaithfulness.

In verse 32, this means that Jesus' use of the word adultery/adulteress could, and perhaps should, be placed inside quotation marks. These marks would alert the reader to the likelihood of Jesus having used some sarcasm, or word play. He would have done this to make his point stronger and broader. Such usage not only fits the immediate context, but it also fits His methods of drawing attention to easily missed principles.

Such usage becomes so very important to the current commentary that it was given its own special number, i.e. "5-A." This usage gives "new" life to several related issues:

- Any unnecessary and lengthy "putting away" by the husband would likely lead to mental or physical adultery by his wife.
- Such "caused" adultery could be narrow, or broad. Today, in the narrow sense, it would include having an affair with another man, (or perhaps even with another woman). In the broader sense it could be "just" an emotional attachment to the voice of Elvis Presley; or, mental love-making with various handsome actors or television personalities.
- Note also that the above adulteries can be done by a husband, who is "caused" to do so, by his wife. He should be stronger (1st Peter 3:7) and less likely to commit such adulteries. However, by the sin of omission, many of today's husbands fail to measure up to 1st Peter.

6. We have now come full circle to the issue of translating the words for porneia and moicheia, i.e. fornication and adultery. The introductory note mentioned not only their closeness to each other but also their individual meanings.

However, as one leaves their fleshly interpretation, the lines blur considerably. Jesus would have been well aware of this. Today's reader does not catch it so easily.

Such blurring explains why so many writers have used the two words interchangeably when making applications based upon *reasoning* alone. Awareness of Jesus' word play (or sarcasm) enables us to use not just human reasoning. It also "attaches" us to pertinent textual foundations.

The *reasoning* of believers is often led of the Holy Spirit but gives only two witnesses who are spiritually related to one another. They are the Christian believer and the Holy Spirit. The third, and independent, witness is found with a "broadened" attachment to the textual foundation.

7. Now let's go back to the Old Testament man who "put his wife away," for good cause, such as venereal disease from another man. Such an Old Testament husband may have just wanted to wait until she was "clean" enough to resume normal marital relations. The Old Testament Jew was deeply involved with matters of the clean and unclean. (See Leviticus chapter 15 and Numbers ch. 5). A kind hearted Old Testament husband may not even have considered divorce—especially for a first offense.

A New Testament husband may wait for a "clean" body, and a clean heart. In the meantime he is not guilty of causing his wife to commit adultery. She remains in her state of adultery—until cleansed in both body and mind.

8. A related conjecture might be helpful now--especially if it were to be provably true. This writer has found no evidence for it in any commentary. On the other hand, Bible culture does not seem to preclude this conjecture. It is about when to issue that certificate of divorce.

An unclean, Jewish husband might cause his wife to become unclean. Hypocritically, he could still divorce her. On the other hand he might not want her next husband to find her with some "uncleanness." Her new husband might suspect that her former husband was the cause of his wife's uncleanness. Therefore the first husband would not issue a certificate of divorce while his wife had some physical uncleanness. He would wait until the uncleanness was gone; and then issue the certificate.

This situation would also make the certificate of divorce especially important to the woman. Without it she would have a greatly reduced chance of finding a new husband. The certificate of divorce did at least these two things for her: first, it kept her from the risk of being stoned for adultery; and second, it gave her what we today might refer to as a "warranty." This may seem crass but it also seems to be in tune with those times.

9. In an Old or New Testament case, the wife who is not caused by her husband to commit adultery, may still make her own choice to become martially unfaithful. In cases like this, she cannot be caused to become an adulterous woman...! She already is one! In these cases, the NIV makes no sense at all.

Again we give one serious caution: the husband who "cuts off" his wife (or "puts her away") risks being in sin for causing her adultery. This could easily be the case when she has generally been a very good wife to him, including not being unfaithful in any way.

10. Finally, we now list another case of what looks like male chauvinism. The NIV translators appear to show Jesus allowing the husband to divorce his wife for unfaithfulness. She then is never "re-marriageable." The man may or may not be "re-marriageable." This makes Jesus look bad. That does not make good sense. If, on the other hand, we use the KJV, Wuest, or the corrected NIV, good sense is right there in front of us.

2nd and 3rd Cases Impact> Divorce and Remarriage

1. In the NIV, the husband may remarry, depending on how one interprets later passages—such as those found in 1st Corinthians chapter 7.

2. In the NIV, an inverted reading would state, "...anyone who divorces his wife—not for marital unfaithfulness—causes her to become an adulteress...." Therefore, the divorcee' who was not divorced for marital unfaithfulness, automatically becomes an adulteress (if she remarries). And this writer says, "Go figure...."

Consider the silliness of this related example for a wife who could not have children. If her husband divorced her, and if she remarried, she would be guilty of adultery. And now we have a double "go figure...." The NIV is just not making good sense.

Her solution might be to make certain her divorce was for marital unfaithfulness. Then she could remarry and not be guilty of adultery. That's a triple "go figure...."

One slight support for the NIV thinking might have been based upon divorce proceedings from the last century. It was then common for the certificate of divorce to list the cause. If it was adultery, at least the next potential husband would know what he was getting. Why not just use a cattle branding iron and burn the letter "A" into the skin of her forehead? And what if her husband had been the root cause of whatever adultery she committed? Would he also get branded? What about a branding for mental adultery? How can we do that? Would a lobotomy suffice?

3. In the NIV, it would appear that any man who marries any divorced woman becomes an adulterer. Some have tried to take away the impact of this situation by saying that only the first act of marriage is adultery, and that afterwards the marriage is normal. Why not keep it simple, and find a correct translation?

4. If we say that such adultery only applies when the divorced woman was not divorced for unfaithfulness, we create another problem. An "innocent" wife, divorced by a hardhearted husband, is not able to remarry without being a sinner. This too is silly.

5. The NIV, and many other modern translations have sewn shut the opportunity for most divorced persons to have a second chance at marriage without being labeled adulterous. This is wrong, and their study Bibles could at least make notes to recognize this.

6. Again this writer prays for those who will be '*Converted by Callison,*' or by Wuest, or by Richards, or by the work done in this survey of Scriptural divorces.

[4th] *Case> Matthew 19:3*

KJV - 3 The Pharisees also came unto him, tempting him, and saying unto him, Is it lawful for a man to [4] PUT AWAY his wife for every cause?

Wuest – 3 And there came to Him Pharisees, putting Him to the test and saying, Is it lawful for one to [4] dismiss his wife for every cause?

NIV - 3 Some Pharisees came to him to test him. They asked, "Is it lawful for a man to [4] divorce his wife for any and every reason?"

NIV corrected - 3 Some Pharisees came to him to test him. They asked, "Is it lawful for a man to [4] ~~divorce~~ put away his wife for any and every reason?"

4th Case> Commentary

1. Most commentators agree that the Pharisees were trying to put Jesus between a rock and a hard place. That is between the school of Hillel and the school of Shammai. One was liberal and the other was conservative. Jesus instead pointed them to how the Creator has always wanted marriage to be, i.e. permanent (and peaceful).

2. Either divorce or "putting away, permanently" would interfere with that plan of the Creator; so, translation choice here is not overly important.

3. It may be worth noting that the NIV, being a dynamic equivalent translation, used a word that is the common result of today's marriages that get into trouble. On the other hand, if the NIV (and other modern translations) would use "put away" or some equivalent, it might show forth that interim step which should occur before divorce. Perhaps the use of the term put away (or separate) could help prevent many divorces....

4. Here might be a good place to state that in modern times the words for husband and wife can effectively be interchanged in any of the applications in this chapter. Women today in America have just as much access to divorce, as did the men back in Jesus' day, or in Moses' time. This is not necessarily a good thing. It may be a necessary thing for wives whose husbands lack any fear of God. But what about when both spouses lack any fear of God? Will this not lead to annihilation of the family?

4th Case> Impact on Divorce and Remarriage

Just one notation comes to mind. The NIV, as good as it is, could be better--if it would state "put away," or "separate." As stated above, this might help prevent many divorces--by highlighting some interim term and not jumping so quickly to say divorce. That would seem to be a more sensible way to apply the word "apoluo."

[5th, 6th, 7th, and 8th] *Cases> Matthew 19:7, 8 & 9*

KJV - 7 They say unto him, Why did Moses then command to give a writing of divorcement, and to [5] PUT HER AWAY? 8 He saith unto them, Moses because of the hardness of your hearts suffered you to [6] PUT AWAY your wives: but from the beginning it was not so. 9 And I say unto you, Whosoever shall [7] PUT AWAY his wife, except it be for fornication, and shall marry another, committeth adultery: and whoso marrieth her which is [8] PUT AWAY doth commit adultery.

Wuest - 7 They say to Him, Why then did Moses command to give her a bill of divorce and [5] dismiss her? He says to them, Moses, on account of the hardness of your heart permitted you to [6] dismiss your wives. But from the beginning it (namely, the right of divorce) has not been thus, right down to the present moment, and as a result it continues to be at variance with the original enactment. Moreover, I am saying to you, Whoever [7] dismisses his wife for any other cause than fornication, and marries [8] another, is committing adultery. [The above stated "right" of divorce is enclosed by brackets in the Wuest Translation. Such bracketing can indicate postulation. An improved postulation would be, "the responsibility of divorce."]

NIV - 7 "Why then," they asked, "did Moses command that a man give his wife a certificate of divorce and [5] send her away?" 8 Jesus replied, "Moses permitted you to [6] divorce your wives because your hearts were hard. But it was not this way from the beginning. 9 I tell you that anyone who [7] divorces his wife, except for marital unfaithfulness, and marries [8] another woman, commits adultery."

NIV corrected - 7 "Why then," they asked, "did Moses command that a man give his wife a certificate of divorce and [5] send her away?" 8 Jesus replied, "Moses permitted you to [6] ~~divorce~~ put away your wives because your hearts were hard. But it was not this way from the beginning. 9 I tell you that anyone who [7] ~~divorces~~ puts away his wife, except for marital unfaithfulness, and marries [8] another woman commits adultery."

5th thru 8th Cases> Commentary

1. First, is a note that not too much should be made of the interplay between the words "command" and "permit." In Mark chapter ten, this interplay is in reverse order.

2. Wuest postulates "the right of divorce." It would have been better to state, "the responsibility of divorce." A right is often used primarily for self. A responsibility is more likely to be used within the will of God—for others, and for self....

2. As Wycliffe Commentary, and others have noted, the certificate of divorce was for the protection of the wife and not for the whimsical use of the husband. The Bible shows a pattern of God taking care of the un-empowered when they are being oppressed. If her husband no longer wanted her, for good reasons or bad ones, she could at least find another husband—if she had that certificate.

3. Notice that Jesus did not speak of the certificate of divorce—even though the Pharisees spoke specifically about it, and the action of "putting away." This could appear to be a subtle difference, but this difference could also change the entire interpretation of this passage. Earlier in this same passage (19:3-6), Jesus avoided the question of the same Pharisees—and headed for higher ground. Why shouldn't we deduct that He is again taking the listener to higher ground?

4. If Jesus is taking higher ground, then He is avoiding discussion of divorce and the certificate that legalizes it. Jesus appears to be willing to discuss "putting away," but His words omit the word for certificate (of divorce). This would mean that the NIV's use of the word divorce is wrong, and that the KJV, Wuest, and the NIV-corrected are giving a better interpretation. This also makes better sense in view of the context and method of His debate and purposes as a teacher.

5. This writer believes that the largest issue here is hardheartedness; also implying "cruelty" (per Adam Clarke), and destitute of spiritual perception (Strong's).

Jesus had already said that He had not come to do away with one jot or tittle of the Law. The Law was there to aid in divorce when and if a marital relationship was in failure. The wife may have been the initial and ongoing cause, or the husband may have been. One may have started it and the other one may have decided to finish it. Peace had always been an overriding issue.

When hardheartedness, cruelty, or spiritual emptiness on the part of either spouse (or both spouses) continued for too long, a certificate of divorce was God's solution. It is worth noting here that God must have had the children in mind too. He most likely would not have wanted them to live too long in a "war zone."

6. From *2nd and 3rd Cases> Commentary (Matthew 5:32)*: numbers 3, 4, 5 & 6 also apply now. The same issue, of "put away" except for marital unfaithfulness, was in view for the 2nd and 3rd cases (above).

5th thru 8th Cases> Impact on Divorce and Remarriage

1. From *2nd and 3rd Cases> Impact on Divorce and Remarriage*: numbers 1 thru 5 also apply now; similar issues were in view....

2. Logic professors name "repeated assertion" as a potential error in logic. In regard to impacts 1 thru 5, the average reader of the NIV now has two places telling him about how remarriage can be adulterous. If the NIV is right, then that is a good thing. However, if the NIV is wrong, then that is a bad thing. Obviously this writer perceives the NIV to be wrong, in this area.

The NIV is truly a wonderful translation in most other areas, and it is my favorite translation. One wishes that they would fix, or at least annotate, this one major error--with appropriate corrections or comment.

[9th, 10th, 11th, and 12th] *Cases> Mark 10:2, 4, 11, & 12*

KJV - 2 And the Pharisees came to him, and asked him, Is it lawful for a man to [9] PUT AWAY his wife? tempting him.
3 And he answered and said unto them, What did Moses command you?
4 And they said, Moses suffered to write a bill of divorcement, and to [10] PUT HER AWAY.
5 And Jesus answered and said unto them, For the hardness of your heart he wrote you this precept.
6 But from the beginning of the creation God made them male and female.
7 For this cause shall a man leave his father and mother, and cleave to his wife;
8 And they twain shall be one flesh: so then they are no more twain, but one flesh.
9 What therefore God hath joined together, let not man put asunder.
10 And in the house his disciples asked him again of the same matter.
11 And he saith unto them, Whosoever [11] shall PUT AWAY his wife, and marry another, committeth adultery against her.
12 And if a woman shall [12] PUT AWAY her husband, and be married to another, she committeth adultery.

Wuest - 2 And having come to Him, Pharisees kept on asking Him whether it is lawful for a man to [9] dismiss a wife, putting Him to the test. And He answering, said to them, What did Moses command you? And they said, Moses permitted a writing of a bill of divorce and to [10] dismiss her. And Jesus said to them, On account of your hardheartedness he wrote this commandment for you. [Verses 6, thru 8 are omitted; they are similar to the KJV.] That therefore which God yoked together, let no man separate. And in the house again the disciples kept on asking Him concerning this. And He says to them, Whoever [11] puts away his wife and marries another woman commits adultery against her. And if she herself, having [12] put away her husband, marries another man, she commits adultery.

NIV - 2 Some Pharisees came and tested him by asking, "Is it lawful for a man to [9] divorce his wife?"

3 "What did Moses command you?" he replied.

4 They said, "Moses permitted a man to write a certificate of divorce and [10] send her away."

5 "It was because your hearts were hard that Moses wrote you this law," Jesus replied. 6 "But at the beginning of creation God 'made them male and female.' 7'For this reason a man will leave his father and mother and be united to his wife, 8 and the two will become one flesh.' So they are no longer two, but one. 9 Therefore what God has joined together, let man not separate."

10 When they were in the house again, the disciples asked Jesus about this. 11 He answered, "Anyone who [11] divorces his wife and marries another woman commits adultery against her. 12 And if she [12] divorces her husband and marries another man, she commits adultery."

NIV corrected - 2 Some Pharisees came and tested him by asking, "Is it lawful for a man to [9] ~~divorce~~ put away his wife?"

3 "What did Moses command you?" he replied.

4 They said, "Moses permitted a man to write a certificate of divorce and [10] send her away."

5 "It was because your hearts were hard that Moses wrote you this law," Jesus replied. 6 "But at the beginning of creation God 'made them male and female.' 7'For this reason a man will leave his father and mother and be united to his wife, 8 and the two will become one flesh.' So they are no longer two, but one. 9 Therefore what God has joined together, let man not separate."

10 When they were in the house again, the disciples asked Jesus about this. 11 He answered, "Anyone who [11] ~~divorces~~ puts away his wife and marries another woman commits adultery against her. 12 And if she [12] ~~divorces~~ puts away her husband and marries another man, she commits adultery."

9th thru 12th Cases> Commentary

1. These cases are so similar to those in Matthew 19 that their basic commentary does not need repeating. The verses themselves are also quite similar. Mark does add the possibility of a wife "putting away" her husband and marrying another man.... Matthew and Luke do not address this but the principles and outcomes are the

same.... Mark is apparently showing Jesus' awareness of some Gentile women being able to accomplish a legal divorce. By the Law of Moses, Jewish women were not afforded this privilege, or protection.

2. One brand new deduction is now taken, from Mark. (It was available in Matthew but not discussed.) In verse 4, he talks about "writing a certificate of divorce" and also about another, distinct action. This other action is *"to put her away"* in the KJV, *"to dismiss her"* in Wuest, and *"to send her away'"* in the NIV.

"Good" logic would ask, "Why not write a certificate of divorce, and divorce her? Or, "Why not write her a certificate of dismissal, and dismiss her?" Or, "Why not write her a certificate of put away, and put her away. Or finally, "Why not write her a certificate of send away, and send her away?" Sorry for the carrying on here, but it is important to the whole issue of "applying apoluo."

Apparently "apoluo" is definably different from a certificate of divorce—regardless of how it is translated into English. This deduction adds a lot of favorable weight to the whole proposition of this chapter and book!

3. One indirect, "new" issue also arises. In Mark, Jesus answers a question of the Pharisees with, "What did Moses <u>command</u> you?" The Pharisees retorted with Moses <u>permitted</u>.... In the *opposite order*, Matthew shows the Pharisees asking why did Moses <u>command?</u>; and Jesus replying that, "Moses <u>permitted</u>...("putting away").

Matthew and Mark may have reported on two different parts of the same "debate," on the same day. In the first debate, perhaps by Matthew, Jesus may have been correcting the Pharisees by reminding them that Moses was giving "a permission" but not a command. In the second debate, Mark may have been showing Jesus to be baiting the Pharisees to see what they would do or say. They appear to give a correct response by telling Jesus that Moses permitted putting away...but did not command it. This would fit the overall context of what we have learned about Jesus calling folks to higher ground, and His occasional effort to cause, or allow, the Pharisees to fall into their own trap.

[13th and 14th] *Cases> Luke 16:18*

KJV - 18 Whosoever [13] PUTTETH AWAY his wife, and marrieth another, committeth adultery: and whosoever marrieth her that is [14] PUT AWAY from her husband committeth adultery.

Wuest – 18 Everyone who [13] dismisses his wife and marries another commits adultery. And he who marries her who has been [14] dismissed from a husband commits adultery.

NIV - 18 "Anyone who [13] divorces his wife and marries another woman commits adultery, and the man who marries a [14] divorced woman commits adultery.

NIV corrected - 18 "Anyone who [13] ~~divorces~~ puts away his wife and marries another woman commits adultery, and the man who marries a [14] ~~divorced~~ put away woman commits adultery.

13th and 14th Cases> Commentary

1. Luke gives basically the same information as already addressed in Matthew 5:32 and Mark 10:11. There is no need to repeat it.

2. It may be worth noting that Luke's one verse on the issues at hand is without much directly related context. His words, as used in the NIV, also add to the likelihood that the casual Bible reader would use them to stop all remarriage to a divorced woman. Again this just does not make good sense—it shows Jesus to be chauvinist. The word of God almost always shows leadership as the man's responsibility, but it seldom does so at the expense of an otherwise "innocent" woman.

3. The reader may have noticed my cases add up to fourteen whereas Callison's added up to eleven. This is probably due to a finer breakdown of occurrences. For example, the one verse Matthew 19:9 uses the term "put away" twice in the same sentence; as does Luke 16:18.

Summary of Matthew, Mark & Luke -with Jesus involved

1. Matthew has the most usages of "apoluo"—with eight, Mark is second—with four, and Luke is last—with two. Matthew is known to have been aiming largely at Jewish listeners, so it would make sense for the most occurrences to be found in his gospel. One wonders why John did not at least mention the issue.

2. Matthew (19:6) and Mark (10:9) both mention Jesus statement about whatever God has joined together, man should not separate. The Greek word for separate is "chorizo." Strong's (5563) defines it thusly: to place room between, ...to go away; and KJV—depart, put asunder, separate. Jesus could have used the Greek word for divorce, i.e. apostasion, but He did not.

This is mentioned because we again see that Jesus avoids the use of the word "divorce." Divorce would happen but He was not going to speak of it, or the bill of divorcement. Each time that the Pharisees brought up the bill of divorcement, Jesus refused to speak directly of it. That writ is also an entirely different word (from "put away"), in the Hebrew. It is noteworthy that Jesus is not found letting the words for the writ come out of His mouth. This seems to be one more way of proving mutual exclusivity between the words for divorce, and "put away." In the Greek, "apoluo" is not "apostasion," and vice versa. In the Hebrew, "shalach" is not "keriythuwth," and vice versa.

Please be reminded that Jesus came not to do away with one jot or tittle of the law (Mt 5:17-18). Just because his lips did not speak of divorce, does not mean that the certificate of divorce was being abandoned. He had not come to abolish the law but to fulfill it. His way of making it fuller was to head for higher, more loving ground. For those who could not make higher ground, the lower ground was still a good place to go.

3. The King James Version and the New International Version have been used mostly because they have the widest acceptance and usage of any Bibles today. Wuest

has been used mostly because of what this unique translation brings to the issues at hand. His work is well named. It does translate and expand--giving us a full(er) meaning of the Greek.

The case of Joseph> Matthew 1:19

KJV - 18 Now the birth of Jesus Christ was on this wise: When as his mother Mary was espoused to Joseph, before they came together, she was found with child of the Holy Ghost. 19 Then Joseph her husband, being a just man, and not willing to make her a publick example, was minded to PUT HER AWAY privily.

Wuest - Now the birth of Jesus was thus. After His mother Mary was promised in marriage to Joseph, before they came together as husband and wife, she was found to be pregnant, the source of that pregnancy being the Holy Spirit. However, Joseph, her husband, being a conscientious, law-abiding man and yet not proposing to make her a public example, after mature consideration desired to dismiss her secretly

NIV - 18 This is how the birth of Jesus Christ came about: His mother Mary was pledged to be married to Joseph, but before they came together, she was found to be with child through the Holy Spirit. 19 Because Joseph her husband was a righteous man and did not want to expose her to public disgrace, he had in mind to divorce her quietly.

NIV corrected - 18 This is how the birth of Jesus Christ came about: His mother Mary was pledged to be married to Joseph, but before they came together, she was found to be with child through the Holy Spirit. 19 Because Joseph her husband was a righteous man and did not want to expose her to public disgrace, he had in mind to ~~divorce~~ put her away quietly.

The case of Joseph> Commentary

1. This "case" was not numbered (as #15) because it does not involve Jesus as a speaker, or "player" in conversation with others. It is well worth listing anyway, because of what it helps to prove about *'Applying "Apoluo." '*

2. As a righteous man, Joseph would have known of the need to give a bill of divorcement--if he were planning a divorce. No mention is made of this in the text. Therefore Joseph appears not to have been considering divorce.

3. A righteous man, like Joseph, would not have been hardhearted. The writ of divorce would not likely have been needed (or used) by Joseph.... He would more likely have been inclined to work out whatever it took to keep his betrothed wife.

4. The Greek word applied to Joseph's considerations is "apolusai," Strong's #630--for "put away."

5. "We" therefore have another strong proof that "put away" is different from divorce, and that the King James

Version applies "apoluo" correctly, to read "put away" (but not divorce).

6. Righteousness in regard to Bible translators should be discussed before leaving this commentary on Joseph. Translators have used various terms to describe Joseph's character: law-abiding, conscientious, just (the actual Greek word), righteous, honorable, good, etc. This writer believes that the NIV has it best, with "righteous."

Joseph's righteousness was not a robe that he wore. He simply was righteous. Commentators have sizeable disagreements about what it means to be righteous. One example favored by this writer is about Zechariah and his wife Elizabeth. In Luke 1:6, the NIV says, "...both of them were upright in the sight of God, observing all the Lord's commandments and regulations blamelessly. This apparently applied to Joseph.

Translators could easily have taken Joseph's character into consideration when deciding on word choice for what Joseph considered to do about Mary's pregnancy. Perhaps some of them did. Apparently the NIV, and other modern translation committees, did not consider this enough. If they had taken Joseph's character into enough consideration, they would not have used the word divorce.

The case of Joseph> Impact on Divorce and Remarriage

1. If more men (and women) were righteous, the number of divorces would be greatly reduced. The number of times someone was "put away," or cut off from marital niceties, would also drop sharply.

2. A righteous man, who suspects marital infidelity by his wife (or fiancé), does not even allow divorce to enter his mind, when he first becomes suspicious.

3. Righteousness can be equated with Spiritual maturity. This has a lot to do with who should have the children, and is to be given further treatment later in this book.

4. Righteousness was missing for most of the members of the Church at Corinth. Let's look at how that weakness was dealt with by Paul in my last case for applying "apoluo."

Last case (arncha glad?)> 1st Corinthians 7:11 (and 10)

KJV - 10 And unto the married I command, yet not I, but the Lord, Let not the wife depart from her husband: 11 But and if she depart, let her remain unmarried, or be reconciled to her husband: and let not the husband PUT AWAY his wife.

Wuest –[Verse 10 and much of verse 11 omitted due in part to the similarity to the KJV]:
And the husband, let him not be putting away his wife.

NIV - 10 To the married I give this command (not I, but the Lord): A wife must not separate from her husband. 11 But if she does, she must remain unmarried or else be reconciled to her husband. And a husband must not divorce his wife.

NIV corrected - To the married I give this command (not I, but the Lord): A wife must not separate from her husband. 11 But if she does, she must remain unmarried or else be reconciled to her husband. And a husband must not ~~divorce~~ put away his wife.

Last case> Commentary

1. Most commentators are agreed that Paul was talking to married spouses who were both born again believers. They will be referred to later as "real" Christians. You see, Paul's instructions will not have much power or influence upon churchgoers who have not been born from above.

2. Here, we may finally have marriages that were "made in Heaven," i.e. both the husband and wife are true believers--supposedly filled with, and controlled by, the Holy Spirit. Their marriage surely should be permanent, as it has been intended since the beginning.

3. The problem of course arises when one spouse (or both) is less than righteous, i.e. less than fully controlled by the Holy Spirit. Separations are bound to come-whether physical, emotional, financial, social, or spiritual.

4. Much more could be said but we are still focusing on the act of "putting away," not the reasons for this act.

5. A Christian woman should not leave her husband. They should be able "immediately" to work out any

differences that might arise--if they will both just follow the Holy Spirit, or Spirit-led counsel.

6. If she goes against the Word of God and the Holy Spirit, by leaving her husband, she must remain "unmarried," that is, unmarried to someone else besides her husband. If she marries someone else, she is then the wife of two husbands. This makes her an adulterous under the higher New Testament ethic, even if she has no ongoing relations with her first husband. It would also make her guilty of polygamy. This rule was probably also meant to preclude "affairs," or "temporary marriages" as some people reference them today.

The departed wife must not engage in sexual immorality. Remember that "marriage," in the Hebrew, is the joining of flesh. It should also have been the joining of hearts but this did not always happen.

Interestingly enough in the immediately preceding chapter, Paul had spoken—in verse 18—against sexual immorality (NIV), or fornication (KJV). These terms are broad. In today's language, they would include an affair, any number of "one night stands," or just finding a prostitute (male, in this case).

The common thread for such immorality is the joining of flesh—temporary or otherwise (1st Corinthians 6:16). The term "one flesh" comes from the Hebrew. Paul was quoting Genesis 2:24 where a man became "one flesh" with his wife. This consummated their union. They were now "glued" together—to say it in an earthy manner.

The separated Christian wife was not to become "glued" to any other man. She was to remain *unmarried,* that is, "un-glued," or else...be reconciled to her husband.

There seems to be no other conclusion to be made—in view of these word meanings, and in view of the immediate context. The two sections in focus are only a mere fifteen verses apart.

Here is one last thought about the departed wife. She also must not become *"one heart"* with, or have a *mental affair* with, someone else. She is still married to her husband. In this type of case the Holy Spirit is still trying to make the marriage work. If she knowingly goes against the Holy Spirit in a matter such great importance, she risks the shipwrecking of her entire faith!

7. Now that we have laid the groundwork with the wife, let's go on to the Christian husband. In the NIV, he is told not to divorce his wife. But again the KJV has it right, with "not...put away."

"Put away," as used here in the KJV and Greek, is not the exact same word as in those previous cases numbered 1-14. However, the Greek word *aphiemi* (Strong's #863) used here for "put away," does have almost the same meaning as does "put away" when used in the gospels.

Interestingly, the word "divorce" is not even listed among the many words used to define #863. It seems that the NIV has again "fast forwarded" the husband into divorce proceedings. Why omit a time of separation? It might be used to save a marriage.

8. If the wife (above) does "marry" somebody else, it is proof that she is completely defeated in her Christian walk. Compare also the examples of defeat in the previous chapter 6. This "marriage" could be of the illicit type described in that previous chapter, or it could be a

legal marriage--depending upon the era and culture in which she lived. In America then, the remarriage of a supposed Christian woman could be tantamount to throwing away her salvation experience. This conclusion would of course also depend somewhat on her husband's carnality, or lack thereof.

9. Paul gave a parenthetical comment before this command against departing, and "putting away." He listed the author of that directive as, "not I, but the Lord." Galatians 1:12ff. explains this phenomenon.

10. Bottom line for this last case: For the husband, Wuest puts it best with, "let him not be 'putting away' his wife." Wuest favors, or at least makes room for, repetitions of "putting away." That is to say, it could happen many times and then not happen for a while and then happen again.... This surely cannot be divorce, and we then have another case where the KJV and Wuest make better sense than many of the modern translations.

Last case> Impact on Divorce and Remarriage

1. Real Christians should not separate (in any way), except for a "season" of prayer as described in 1st Corinthians 7:5. They also should not divorce, and remarriage is usually not applicable.

2. Real Christians who separate must remain that way, or get back together....

3. In America today, real Christians, who willingly backslide and go against the Word of God, may easily get a divorce. They may not so easily expect God to allow them into another marriage--at least not with another Christian spouse. The Spirit of God would have them reconcile to their divorced spouse. Of course this is not likely to happen until one, or both, of them is sufficiently delivered from carnality--so as to make it work.

4. Christian divorce is proof that one spouse, or both, is defeated in his (or her) Christian walk. If one spouse is impossible to live with, then temporary separation may be needed. Divorce should not be needed--unless one spouse has destroyed his or her salvation experience....

5. In a previous chapter, a strong point was made about the need to know who was a born again believer and who was not. This issue can be seen as pivotal in regard to divorce. It could be said that unnecessary divorce initiated by a believer is so serious as to risk shipwrecking his or her faith. (See 1st Timothy 1:19-20.)

6. This case is perhaps the strongest one in the New Testament to show that "real Christian" marriages are supposed to be "permanent."

<u>Special note: My admiration for the New International Version</u> is right up there beside the King James Version. My memory verses are in the NIV, and that choice came after much heartfelt prayer.

In this book, my criticism for the NIV is <u>only</u> in regard to that one word they translate as "divorce." The NIV is not alone on this incorrect translation—most other modern translations make the same error—with this one word.

-10-

Consequences for Children

The last, and perhaps most important issue, in the Book of Ezra was the children. They were hardly mentioned but they were given high impact by being part of the last clause of the book. Ezra 10:44 seems to be a lament for the children of divorce. It seems fitting therefore, in this book about *"Divorce as 'Required' by Scripture,"* to end Part I with some treatment of consequences for children of divorce. Several texts will now be considered, one section at a time, going all the way back to Exodus for the first section.

Exodus 21:1-6 (presented in chapter 2)

Divorces required in Exodus 21 could be prevented only by love—love for the boss, the wife, and the children.

If such love were not present, some children were going to lose the only dad they had ever known. This consequence was a two-edged sword.

On the one side, the children would miss their dad because of a natural affection they would have for him. On the other side, the children would apparently be better off without such a man—who did not truly love them.

God has arranged family in order that good, earthly fathers may model love similar to that of the Heavenly Father. Exodus 21 seems to show that God favors the consequence of divorce for children whose fathers do not love them (or their mother, or the job that supports them all). This may seem like a hard teaching to the traditionalist but it is apparently Scriptural, and therefore deserves our consideration.

It would seem that God would rather see a single mother than to have a bad father around to ruin the idea of what fatherhood is supposed to be. Many women over many centuries have unwisely held onto their marriage solely for the sake of the children, and...because that is what the church told them to do. This too has had consequences. Children have grown up with a damaged view of "fatherhood," and a decreased likelihood of ever seeking a relationship with the Heavenly "Father."

Many other women have "wisely" held onto their marriage for the same reasons and were fortunate enough to finally see a changed spouse, who also then learned to love their children. Some of these successes have been accidental. Others have been the result of much prayer. In any case, the blanket rule by so many churches, to "hold on" no matter what, for the sake of children, seems silly in view of Exodus 21:1-6.

Holding onto a marriage, for the sake of the children, is perhaps good advice for beginners. On the other hand, being willing to let go, for the sake of the children's view of fatherhood, is sometimes better for more "mature" spouses. This is especially true when keeping a husband and "father" is likely to seriously damage the view of the Father in Heaven.

One last thought in this section is about the location of the children of divorce. The Hebrew servant may well have lived in the area of his temporary master. He would then have had some chance to see his children if he wanted to, or if they wanted him to.... This would likely have been an aid in his decision to change his heart. It is also likely that some men did change their heart and were able to be reunited with the family they had lost.

Ezra chapters 9 and 10 (presented in chapter 4)

Geography and "nationality" would have been of more serious consequence on children of divorce in Ezra. The issue of foreigners (unbelievers) was not there in Exodus 21; it was there in Ezra. The likelihood of those children ever having both parents again was small.

In the book of Esther, one finds the only way out for the divorces of Ezra. Esther 8:17 (NIV) reads:

> "In every province and in every city, wherever the edict of the king went, there was joy and gladness among the Jews, with feasting and celebrating. And many people of other nationalities became Jews because fear of the Jews had seized them.

Fear of the Jews, as stated above, was not the best reason for converting to Judaism, but it was apparently a worthy reason in that era. It also must have included some respect for the God of the Jews. In any case, foreigners were converted.

This phenomenon would likely have had impact on those foreign wives in Ezra's time. Some of them were probably allowed to stay married—if they were able to show their fear of (or respect for) the Jewish way of living. Such fear (or respect) would also include reverence for the God of their husbands, instead of their own demonic gods and dead idols. Ezra does not speak directly of this phenomenon but during those trials it is likely to have been considered.

One big reason for such consideration would have been the children. Divorces in Ezra would likely have meant a significant geographic separation of the parents. This would have been good for the "purity" of the Israelite community but it would have reduced the chance of the childless parent ever seeing the children again.

Now arises the issue of who got custody of the children. Ezra does not tell us. The many Bible commentaries on my bookshelves do not tell us much.

Customs of those times would suggest that the mothers, who were "evicted," also took the children with them. This would give the consequence of fatherless children....

Another consequence might have been a deep repentance on the part of the then childless fathers. This might have meant their salvation, especially in a time when so many men were so backslidden as to have intermarried in the first place.

In such cases, one could only hope that someday the children would want to find their father. In those cases when they did find him, he might by then be a good, god-fearing Jew. Perhaps in a few cases, some fathers were then able to be used of God for the "saving" of their children.

Psalms 33:11, an important interlude

Bible harmony is a highly valuable tool for interpretation. When two or more interpretations seem possible, Bible harmony often helps show which one is correct or more pertinent to overall Scriptural patterns.

Psalms 33:11 reads, " But the plans of the LORD stand firm forever, the purposes of his heart through all generations. NIV

Attention is now given to this passage because a subtle pattern seems to be emerging about the children. Our survey of consequences on the children is also showing much of God's plans and purposes for the children. Such plans and purposes do not change, but the methods of achieving them do. As we move away from the Old Testament, and into the New Testament, we will see large changes in those methods.

Jesus and the Children

Jesus showed His concern for children by telling His disciples to let the children come to Him. They would have kept the little ones away. This incident shows up right after the discussion of divorce and "put away," in Matthew 19 and Mark 10. These gospels seem to be saying do not forget the children—when you start talking about divorce, or separation (putting away).

Matthew, Mark, and Luke place the children incident in the same chapter as the one-hundred-fold rewards. In the rewards presentations, all three writers include the giving up of children—for the sake of the Kingdom. Other "family give ups" include parents and siblings, but our focus here is on the children.

Marilee Dunker is the daughter of Bob Pierce. He was the founder of World Vision. The book about this ministry is sub-titled *"This One Thing I Do."* It gives many examples of Bob's success based upon his singular focus, on the ministry. Many years later, his daughter Marilyn wrote a book entitled *"Days of Glory, Seasons of the Night."* This book tells the good, and the bad, about Bob's successful ministry—which helped lead to the breakdown of his marriage.... Marilyn seems to say that the ministry was worth it but that there was a terrible high price to pay on the part of Bob's wife and children.

Apparently most of Bob's close friends did not find him to be out of the will of God. Some of them wished that Bob had been closer to the center of God's will in regard to his family. Which side has the inside scoop on what God thought about this? Did God cause, or just allow, the Pearce consequence?

What about those un-famous men who have family breakdowns? What about their children? Marilee Dunker could easily see the great good her dad was doing for the world. Most children of broken families cannot see such good. They live with the consequence of no dad, and with the consequence of not being able to see worthwhile tradeoffs.

One wonders about Pastor Andy Stanley. He is the successful pastor and son of the famous Dr. Charles Stanley. His mother and dad divorced in 2000, after many years of floundering. They had been separated and reunited and separated again. Was their divorce "required" in terms of how Mrs. Stanley looked at it? What about the consequences upon the children? Did one or more of them give up family for the sake of the kingdom of God?

These stories are mentioned for two reasons. One is to show that some of today's successful overseers have had marital breakdowns and still stayed in ministry. The other is to prove that even in well-known cases, the "experts" just do not know for sure whether some "give ups" are for the sake of the kingdom of God, or not. The children have paid a price, but is that okay with God?

One more issue should be addressed here. It is in regard to the subtle change from the Old Testament to the New. In the Old Testament, the children were put into harm's way for at least these three simple reasons:

a. to be out from under the influence of an earthly dad who did not know how to love, or

b. to keep the Israelite community pure and unaffected by idols and foreign gods, or

c. to keep an Israelite man with weak faith from getting any weaker...and being lost to Hell.

In the New Testament, children may be put at risk, if it is for the sake of the kingdom of God. If the kingdom is not threatened, then children are not to be put at risk.

Kingdom threats are both passive and active. They are active when unbelievers interfere with kingdom culture lifestyle. They are passive when a Christian parent fails to do what he (or she) could do for the kingdom. Jesus would have us keep the children in mind but He also would not have us allow the kingdom to suffer loss, whether it be passive or active.

1st Corinthians 7:11 (see last case of previous chapter.)

Believing spouses should not separate. Their separations not only go against this verse but they also damage the children. Perhaps the main consequence for children is the exposure to a broken covenant. Dad & mom had promised till death us do part, and suddenly they are breaking that promise—made before God and witnesses. Children then learn that promises can be broken...even big promises...even when made before God. This can do irreparable damage to children, and God is not likely to let it go unpunished. Those parents are His children and He will have consequences for them. After all, they have taken His name, in vain!

1st Corinthians 7:12-15 (presented in chapter 7)

Here we have what appears to be the most substantial change from Old Testament ways. Here the believer is told to live with the unbeliever—if it can be done peaceably. What about the consequence on the children? It seems as though God is no longer so concerned about that. One wonders why. It seems to me that it is because of the Holy Spirit.

In Old Testament times, only a small percentage of the people are described as having the Holy Spirit. In New Testament times, the Holy Spirit has been poured out generously upon all believers.

God still wants a pure community but apparently finds the believer capable of sustaining that—with the help of the Holy Spirit. God still wants husbands to love their wives, jobs and kids but now allows peaceful, unbelieving husbands to stay married to their believing wives. The children still have negative consequences but positive ones seem to override that.

God seems to be saying that in the Church Age, it is good for children to see a believing parent hang in there with an unbeliever—if the unbeliever is willing to 'live with" the believer on a good believer's terms. The children have the good consequence of practicing how to be around an unbeliever and still keep their faith—with the help of the Holy Spirit.

Another "good" consequence for the children in a marriage between a believer and an unbeliever occurs in those cases when the unbeliever leaves. The children see the believing parent do the dutiful thing, i.e. let go...and allow divorce. The children's faith in God is increased as the rescue of the believing parent occurs. They see the need to be serious about faith, and the consequences for those who are not. They also see the need to avoid such a marriage in the first place.

Last and perhaps most important to these children is the issue of living peaceably together as a family. When peace can be achieved, the family unit is worth keeping together. When it cannot be achieved, God's word says to allow (or cause) separation from the unpeaceful person.

Timothy & Titus (presented in chapter 8)

Timothy & Titus have some good news for biological children. Their fathers who would become overseers must pay careful attention to the children. They must raise them up to be well behaved. This would include the choice of a good Christian wife. In Titus, believing children become letters of recommendation for overseers. Fathers, who seek to become overseers, must also accomplish a long list of other good characteristics– all of which are "child friendly."

Unfortunately, Timothy & Titus have some mixed consequences for children of polygamists and bigamists. If their fathers would seek the office of overseer, then they must divorce all their wives except one (1st Tim 3:2, and Titus 1:6.). In the short run this would be painful for the children. In the long run, it might be an improvement. If each of their mothers can find a husband of their own, then more children would have more time with their father, or stepfather. Also, they would be likely to keep their biological mother, and she would be better off with a husband she did not have to share with other wives.

Finally, for the sake of the kingdom, single men like Paul, can have Spiritual "children" who benefit from the principles of Timothy & Titus. Surely such single men would try to measure up to every necessary thing on the lists of Timothy & Titus. They would want to have their own "children in the faith." They would want these children to be well disciplined. They would choose good under-shepherds, to watch over them while they were somewhere else.

1st Timothy 4:1-3, and ruinous consequences

For the sake of thousands of children, we should probably mention a denomination-wide, ruinous legalism that has apparently propagated pedophilia.

The world's largest Christian denomination forbids its overseers from marrying. This blanket legalism has "come home to roost." Many parishes have lost millions of dollars—to settle with victims of priestly pedophilia. Many innocent children have been "ruined" for life.

The "church" was only trying to make (force) its leaders to be like Paul and Jesus in regard to being unmarried. If only the "church" had been able to support both celibacy <u>and</u> marriage for its overseers....

Appropriate application of some of the principles in 1 Tim 4:1-3 would seemingly have prevented most of the propagated pedophilia. The verses are now presented for the reader's own discernment (underlining supplied):

"The Spirit clearly says that <u>in later times some will</u> abandon the faith and follow deceiving spirits and things taught by demons. 2 Such teachings come through hypocritical liars, whose consciences have been seared as with a hot iron. 3 They <u>forbid people to marry</u> and order them to abstain from certain foods, which God created to be received with thanksgiving by those who believe and who know the truth. NIV

The list could go on but it is time to close this first part of the book. Part Two has specific information about applying Part One to several "real-time" cases—found in the upcoming chapter 11. Part Two also presents chapter 12—which is an extensive list of smaller but pertinent issues related to this book on Scriptural divorce

Part II
Applications and Additional Assertions

-11-

Cases to Compare

"Where the rubber meets the road," is a popular phrase in our time. This phrase makes a good summary for this chapter. About two dozen Scripture "cases" have been addressed in Part I of this book. About two hundred cases, regarding today's husbands & wives, could be addressed in Part II of this book—but time does not permit.... Actually, ten cases will be presented in regard to where the rubber meets the road....

These flesh & blood cases presented now are arranged by category. This is done with the hope of getting round pegs into round holes, and triangular pegs into triangular holes. These cases are suppositional. They are not taken from anyone known to this writer, but they are taken from circumstances known to most of us.

Categories are unusually important for a number of reasons. First is the need to please God by finding a good model for each situation now addressed. Second is the need to give reassurance to husbands & wives that their situation does have a good model—well connected to the Scriptures. Third is the need to give a roadmap to counselors who can then more quickly locate a rectangular hole for a rectangular situation.... Fourth is the perceived need to show that there are many more models, and situations, in need of thoughtful matching then one might imagine.

Categories are organized in several ways. They are divided by religion: Christian Believer, Churchgoer, and Orthodox Jew. They tend to move from the less serious to the more serious. Numbers are added for ease of location. Titles are added for definition. The numbers will continue to rise regardless of sections. This is done to prevent confusion in regard to location.

Two special categories of "solutions" are now identified, for purposes of clear definition, and appropriate respect. They are used in each of the upcoming cases. This has not been done to put one solution down or lift the other up. It has been done to show why at least two types of solutions are needed.

> Traditional Solution - refers to the time-honored practice of keeping a marriage together regardless of circumstances. As previously mentioned, this is usually the best place to start when marriages develop "normal" troubles. Its common success

makes it worthy of much respect. On the other hand, the Traditional Solution has often led to "hidden" failures—made to look like successes.

Triple-base Solution - refers to what has been developed in this book. It is aimed at marriages that have serious, or non-Traditional, problems. The Triple-base solution includes: [a] good pastoral reasoning, [b] proper translation of the words "apostasion" (divorce), and "apoluo" (separate or "put away"), and [c] appropriate use of Bible models that show divorce.

Some caution is also in order before getting down to, "where the rubber meets the road." Any number of categories will have some overlap. In these situations, the idea is to look for the category that is the closest match. As the situations increase in seriousness, they will likely increase in complexity. This means that accuracy of application will likely be less than perfect. Even so, good application with a Triple-base solution is likely to be more exact than ordinary, Traditional applications.

Respect for tradition is still important. Tradition has given us many good starting points. The Traditional Solution could be compared to the annual visit to your doctor. On the other hand, a Triple-base Solution can be compared to what your doctor does when he gives you a referral. He knows that you need a specialist and wisely sends you to see one. Triple-base Solutions are special in the same way. So, "mates, let's have at it."

SECTION ONE – CHRISTIAN BELIEVERS

1. The "Innocent" Spouse, who accepts divorce

1-a. Situation

Ivan & Isabel got married right out of high school. They had been seeing each other for years. They were both leaders in their church's activities. "Everyone" thought they would have a perfect marriage.

Ivan & Isabel had four children. Ivan was a successful farmer and Isabel a wonderful mother. About ten years into their marriage, trouble began.

Ivan got into Internet pornography. He knew it was a sin from day one but he chose not to get help. When he finally went for help, he chose not to follow the strict advice given. The farm work began to slide, as did fathering and husbanding.

Ivan finally abandoned family & farm and church. He found a go-go dancer to live with. Isabel got their pastor to help Ivan but it never went deep enough. Ivan sued Isabel for divorce. Isabel did not want a divorce but was at her wits end, after more than five years of having to try and hold things together with only a thread.

Isabel's church told her to keep hanging on—but they could not pay many of her bills, and seldom offered.... Her health began to suffer, and she could see her health problems increasing in more than one area.

Isabel had a couple of close Christian friends who had helped her during these difficult times. They assured her that she had been a wonderful wife ninety-nine percent of the time. They and the church rightly believed her to be "innocent." Ivan also agreed that Isabel had always been a very good wife and mother. What should Isabel do?

1-b. Traditional Solution

Isabel should refuse to sign off for an easy divorce. Didn't Jesus say that man should not separate what God has put together? She should also try to delay every divorce proceeding that arises. She should even temporarily take time away from her children to fight the divorce. She should just hang in there until some breakdown becomes so serious that her church comes to her rescue—if they ever would, even if they ever could.

1-c. Triple-base Solution

Isabel should "let go" of her husband by agreeing with several Scriptures and by signing off for the divorce sought by her husband. 1st Corinthians 7:15 apparently applies to her husband—he has become an unbeliever.

Ivan may, or may not have ever been a believer. This has much to do with whether the reader supports the doctrine of once saved, always saved. This writer does not support that doctrine. (Refer here to Deuteronomy chapter 31 - verses 6 & 8 as opposed to verse 17; and Jesus' Parable of the Sower, and 2nd Timothy 2:12, etc.)

Exodus 21:1-6 supports Isabel's acceptance of this divorce—in at least two ways. First, Ivan does not love his job, or his wife, or their children; and second, this has been his attitude for a half-dozen years. Moreover, even the patriarch Jacob worked only seven years for Rachel, and seven (more) for Leah (Genesis 29:27).

1-d. Comments & Suggestions

If Isabel is obedient to 1st Corinthians 7:15, and if she is otherwise living for Jesus, she can expect the Lord to return unto her a one-hundred-fold husband.

Isabel and her children would likely also then have a one-hundred-fold father in their new family. It may take a while for the children to accept or understand this.

The children are in need of a good, Christian father—even if he is not their biological father. They will be grown and gone all too soon, and Ivan shows no sign of change—any time soon.

Ivan must face the results of having abandoned his Lord, his church, his livelihood, his wife and their children. It is likely to be better for him in the long run than to be "pampered" any longer.

2. The "Innocent" Spouse, who initiates divorce

2-a. Situation

Consider the same story of Ivan & Isabel, with two changes. First Ivan began to regularly beat Isabel and the children, and second—Ivan would not initiate a divorce suit. Next, Isabel got a protection from abuse order but Ivan was still able to terrorize them "from a distance." He would sneak onto the property, do his damage and get away. His stated purpose for all of this violence was to get Isabel to file for divorce. His acts of violence were also escalating. What should Isabel do in this case?

2-b. Traditional Solution

Isabel would continue with being "separated" from Ivan, and pray more—for him to change his heart. And wait....

2-c. Triple-base Solution

Isabel should file for divorce—unless she and her accountability partners would agree that martyrdom was the will of God for her, and perhaps the children.

"Letting go" of Ivan, in this case, would require Isabel to initiate the divorce proceedings. She would be doing the lesser of two evils—like Shiphrah & Puah in Exodus 21. To save lives, Isabel would have to do what she ordinarily would not do.

2-d. Comments & Suggestions

The Bible avoids a fair amount of Satan's methods. It does not give too many gory details of the Devil's ways. Therefore, Isabel will not find a direct model of what to do. Shiphrah & Puah did not have a direct model either.

When wickedness goes beyond the pages of the Bible, Spirit-led believers may have to do the same. Isabel would be following the principle of doing whatever it takes to try and save the lives of her children, and their mother. If she would fail to act, and eventually be killed by Ivan, who would raise the children? The children would then have lost both parents.

Numbers 30:3-5 states, "When a young woman still living in her father's house makes a vow to the LORD or obligates herself by a pledge 4 and her father hears about her vow or pledge but says nothing to her, then all her vows and every pledge by which she obligated herself will stand. 5 But if her father forbids her when he hears about it, none of her vows or the pledges by which she obligated herself will stand; the LORD will release her because her father has forbidden her." NIV

These Old Testament verses contain an important principle—a father may break the vow of a daughter. It seems to me that this principle "dovetails" with Proverbs 30:21-23 (discussed in chapter five). God's creation will not stand long for a wife who is not loved by her husband. Isabel's Heavenly Father certainly has the authority to break the wedding vow once made in good faith, by Isabel. Things have changed and the Spirit of God may actually urge Isabel to break her wedding vow by initiating a divorce.

3. A Believer Married to an Unbeliever, peacefully

3-a. Situation

Bob the believer married Ursula the unbeliever during their senior year at a Christian college. Bob mistakenly assumed that Ursula was a believer. Ursula herself was not sure whether she was a believer.

Bob & Ursula decided not to have children early in their marriage. They both threw themselves into careers. In the fourth year of their marriage, Ursula unexpectedly got pregnant. They both chose to welcome the new life.

When their son was old enough to begin church life, Bob took him every Sunday. Ursula went only a couple of times a year. Until the baby had come, neither Bob nor Ursula had gone to church much.

Around the age of three, a large disagreement came between Bob & Ursula—about children's videos. Bob did not want their son to watch some of the videos received from his wife's side of the family. Ursula thought Bob was narrow-minded and prudish but chose to honor Bob. His decisions about videos were based on whether they contained God honoring material.

The video issue was only one of many more to come. Dad and mom spent a lot of time deciding what honored God. It got even harder when their son was about eight years old and wanted to know whether Jesus was the only way to Heaven.

Bob became weary of the many discussions—even though Ursula's track record was very good in terms of honoring his leadership. Bob decided to ask his pastor about getting out of the marriage. What should the pastor tell him?

3-b. Traditional Solution

Pastor tells Bob to stick it out—it could be much worse.... He also tells Bob to make as many compromises with Ursula as possible—so that their son would have more parts of both parents' personalities.

3-c. Triple-base Solution

Pastor tells Bob that there is a specific word for him in 1st Corinthians 7:12-16. Bob is to stay with the marriage because it is peaceful—relatively speaking. The pastor tells Bob to make very few compromises on Christian, or moral, issues. He tells Bob that it is his responsibility to raise the son to be a Christian. He further tells Bob & Ursula that this is the will of God for their family.

3-d. Comments & Suggestions

This case may seem like too much idealism. It has been somewhat abbreviated for sake of presentation. In actual life, it likely would not be so easy. Nevertheless, the principles given are in the Word of God and should be put forward as much as possible.

4. *A Believer Married to an Unbeliever, "un-peacefully"*

4-a. Situation

Take the same couple—Bob & Ursula—and make a few changes. Ursula becomes contentious on a regular basis. Ursula lets their son watch terrible things by video and on television. Ursula makes Sunday mornings a pain for everybody—in hopes that Bob will give up on church. Ursula uses marital relations (sex) to manipulate many decisions. Bob gets to his wits end and goes to his pastor for advice. What should he be told?

4-b. Traditional Solution

Pastor tells Bob to stick it out—it could be worse. He tries to counsel with Ursula but she refuses. He tells Bob that, like it or not, he will have to make some compromises to save his marriage.

4-c. Triple-base Solution

Pastor tells Bob that he basically has three choices. [1] hang in there and pray for improvement, [2] hang in there but do not make too many compromises—even if it means that she gets angry enough to divorce him, [3] do not hang in there any longer; initiate divorce—based upon the fact that Ursula is not willing to live peacefully with Bob.

4-d. Comments & Suggestions

Again the case has been somewhat simplified but there is not much need to describe it further. The issues are clear and the Scripture is too (1st Corinthians 7:12-16).

It will ultimately boil down to Bob's decision. One would hope that Bob would have a team of prayer partners—who would help him with his decision.

It is worth taking note that the "specialist" approach, afforded by the Triple-base method, also offers Bob the freedom to grow or to remain static in his Christian walk. In either case, Bob is not likely to see the Lord as an unmerciful warden. This should make Bob more likely to want to become a complete disciple of Christ.

The "un-peaceful" home is likely having a very bad influence on the child. It will be a shame if divorce has to happen. However, the long-term result on such a child being raised in a "war zone" would be even worse. God has called us to live in peace—1st Corinthians 7:15(b).

SECTION TWO - CHURCHGOERS

5. *Churchgoers Marry, later on he is born again*

5-a. Situation

Charles' parents and Carol's parents have been good family people all their life. Charles and Carol have always gone to church. Charles & Carol have a lovely church wedding. Charles & Carol continue going to church—but it is only one of several "good habits."

One day Charles is influenced by a fellow worker to accept Jesus Christ as his personal savior. Charles is born from above and filled with the Holy Spirit.

Church is no longer a habit—but a hunger. Charles decides to go beyond Sunday morning worship times. He is reasonable, but Carol is reluctant.... Charles ends up going to many church activities without Carol. She does not try to deter her husband from his new life in Christ, but she does wonder about it.

The marriage of Charles & Carol remains peaceful but Charles feels an increasing marital emptiness due to his increasing spirituality. Charles reads about how the apostle Paul wished for all men to be single, and goes to his pastor for advice about this. What should he be told?

5-b. Traditional Solution

Charles would be told to remain in his marriage, regardless of what happens. He & Carol would be invited to counseling about the marital emptiness being felt by Charles.

5-c. Triple-base Solution

Charles would be told to remain in his marriage, for as long as Carol would peacefully "live with" him. Charles should be warned not to create any unnecessary "distance" between himself and his wife. He should also be counseled about the possibility of Carol losing interest in the marriage. He should find some accountability partners to help him continue as a faithful husband.

Charles should pray for Carol to become a Christ follower but he should not manipulate her in this direction. Charles should be told about what he might do if Carol turns the marriage into an un-peaceful one. He must continually make many extra efforts to make sure that he is not doing anything un-peaceful.

5-d. Comments & Suggestions

If Charles walks the good Christian walk, and if Carol tries to stop him, Charles may need to make some changes. His Bible options, as led by the Holy Spirit, would include celibacy, separation, or divorce.

6. Churchgoers Marry, later on she is born again

6-a. Situation

Consider the same Charles & Carol (above) but that she is the spouse that gets born again. In this case, immediate trouble comes into their marriage. Charles becomes a thorn to Carol, in every aspect of their marriage. She chooses to suffer silently until sexual perversion is proposed by Charles. He wants to have some of their old friends, and some of his new ones, over to their home for an orgy. He has also been "forcing" her into unnatural acts of sex. What should Carol do?

6-b. Traditional Solution

Hang in there but do not go along with orgies and unnatural sex acts. You married him, for better or worse, and this "worseness" is not likely to go on forever.

6-c. Triple-base Solution

Make immediate arrangements to separate from Charles. Give him time to straighten out his life. If he does, then be sure that his doctor gives him a clean bill of health before getting back together. If he does not get his life straightened out, then seek a divorce.

6-d. Comments & Suggestions

The tragic issue of venereal disease, aids, etc. might as well be brought up now. Carol should also have herself tested for any such infections. If she has gotten something from Charles, he should be confronted about it. This would not necessarily have to be done by Carol.

The confrontation would be for a couple of reasons. First, so that Charles might know what disease he might have. Second, to let him know that others may have to be told—for the sake of their health. Third, to let him know how serious the risk is of the marriage being almost over.

It seems time again to mention that rare option of martyrdom. If Carol responsibly believes that death is something God would have her risk, then she may do so. She would need to submit her belief to several close and mature Christians before going through with it. In this case she might choose not to separate from Charles....

7. Churchgoers Marry, later both are born again

7-a. Situation

Larry & Laura have a typical churchgoer's marriage. They attend worship two or three times a month and are involved in a couples' group. They share leadership equally in all marriage related matters.

Larry & Laura go to a Billy Graham Crusade and make the trip down front to receive Jesus Christ as their personal Savior. They both become deeply interested in the Bible and use it morning & evening for devotions.

They read various Christian books about marriage. One of these books helps them both to see the need for Larry to be the primary leader in their home. He does learn to do a rather good job with this responsibility. But sometimes he overdoes the "headship thing. "

When Laura will not do what Larry wants, he will not be sociable with her. She tells him about this and they even counsel with their care group leader. What should the care group leader tell them?

7-b. Traditional Solution

Laura should hang in there until Larry further matures and gets over his misuse of power.

7-c. Triple-base Solution

Larry should be told that he is "putting away," or separating from his wife—in the social arena of their marriage. Larry should be told that the word of God forbids him from doing this (1st Corinthians 7:11-b).

They both should be shown how modern translations of the Bible miss this point—due to saying divorce instead of "put away," or separate. They could be advised that this is one of the only major blunders by modern translations. Also, the King James Version is not without a blunder or two of its own.

7-d. Comments & Suggestions

Larry & Laura might do themselves a favor with the purchase of a Parallel Bible—King James Version in one column, with the New International Version right beside it. A good commentary might also be advisable.

8. *Churchgoers, married but masking success*

8-a. Situation

Harry and Harriet are both hardhearted but they are the only ones who know it. Harry "puts away" Harriet and she does the same to him. He withholds his paycheck. She has let herself become obese to get even with him. He insists on going to church but complains all afternoon—till Harriet has to leave the room. She makes fun of his job and salary. If he doesn't like a dinner she had put on the table, he orders in some pizza. They do finally visit their pastor.

8-b. Traditional Solution

Harry and Harriet get into long term counseling with their pastor and about half of their problems go away. They are told to hang in there and keep working on improvements.

8-c. Triple-base Solution

Harry and Harriet are taken thru a Bible study about hardheartedness—as addressed in the gospels. They are shown, thru the King James Version, that "putting away" one's spouse is usually the result of a cold heart. They are further told that they need the infilling of the Holy Spirit—as the only true cure for their problems.

8-d. Comments & Suggestions

Harry and Harriet will find help with both solutions (above). However, as they would fall back into their sins of hardheartedness, they should be reminded of their need to have the love of Jesus in their hearts. Even after they would accept Christ into their hearts, a lot of work would still need to be done....

SECTION THREE - ORTHODOX JEWS

9. "Innocent" Wife, being put away

9-a. Situation

Rueben & Rachel have been married for about ten years. Rueben has gotten bored with their marriage and has found a mistress. Rueben refuses to give Rachel a bill of divorcement because he cannot name any major failure by Rachel. His personal problem is simply that he wants new adventure with another woman. What can Rachel do?

9-b. Traditional Solution

Rachel must live with the situation. Jewish women believers have no right (or responsibility) to initiate a divorce.

9-c. Triple-base Solution

Rachel could try to convince Rueben that God hates it when a husband "puts away" his wife (without a certificate of divorce, as required in Deuteronomy 24:1). She could also use Malachi 2:16 with a correct translation of the Hebrew word "shalach."

Since she and Rueben respect Jesus as a great teacher, she could even try to show how Jesus addressed the issues of hardheartedness and "putting away."

9-d. Comments & Suggestions

Rachel may have to give up some of her orthodoxy and initiate her own divorce. This will mean that she will likely not find an orthodox Jewish man for a second husband. Perhaps she would be better off with a lesser orthodox man anyway....

10. *"Guilty" Wife, put away temporarily*

10-a. Situation

Simon & Sarah have been married for about five years. Both have been "running around" on each other. Simon has been very careful but Sarah has not. She has contracted a serious venereal disease. They both decide to stop all acts of unfaithfulness. Simon further decides to separate himself conjugally from Sarah until she is well again. She gets well but Simon continues to "put her away." What can she do?

10-b. Traditional Solution

Sarah has no choice but to hang in there.

10-c. Triple-base Solution

Same as with Rachel (above). Also, Sarah could try to convince Simon that he deserved to be "put away" just as much as she did. Perhaps this would soften his heart before God and his wife.

10-d. Comments & Suggestions

Sarah should wait for a year or two and reevaluate her situation. If Simon continues to "put her away," she may need to consider the same options as Rachel (above).

Chapter Closing Cautions

The cases in this chapter have obviously not been able to cover the hundreds of different situations of serious marital difficulty. My hope is that the ten cases above have shown the reader how important it is to make direct use of the word of God. It is also important to use a correct translation—especially in regard to divorce, versus "put away."

Another hope is that the reader can now clearly see the great contrast between the Traditional Solution, and the Triple-base Solution. Caution should always be a concern when either one of these solutions is used with no consideration of the other.

The upcoming, last chapter is designed to address more issues—indirectly related to where the rubber meets the road. These issues often cause small but noticeable adjustments in the handling of actual cases.

Note of Invitation—There may come a time when this book will be expanded into a new edition. Interested persons may submit their own short stories for consideration in such a new edition. A "publisher" address may be found near the front of this book, on page iv.

-12-

Book Closing "Bits"

This last chapter is designed to catch a number of issues too small to have their own chapter. They will be presented bit by bit—each bit being underlined. You may compare these bits to a buffet at a restaurant. Some bits will be tasty and easily digested, while others may be chewy and a bit salty. They all have some impact on the issues already presented in this book. They are listed in alphabetical order in the *Table of Contents.*

Bits "Buffet"

1. God's will has appeared in some cases, in this book, to be multiple. Actually, God has a variety of solutions to most any problem. One useful way to consider His solutions is to divide them into two major categories.

(Further narrowing can also be done within these two major categories.)

a. First is the perfect will of God. A loving and peaceful marriage for a whole lifetime is in this category. Compare also the Garden of Eden or Israel before she had kings.

b. Second is the permissive will of God. Moses did permit a man to "put away" his wife, and did require a writ of divorce if such "putting away" was to be permanent. Compare here the giving of kings to the Israelites. They wanted Kings—God did not—but He permitted this anyway.

2. Christian maturity, or the lack of it, has major impact on finding the "higher" will of God. It of course has major impact on many of the issues in this book. Christian maturity comes in three basic varieties:

a. Immature "babes" in Christ. These are described by Paul in 1st Corinthians 3:1-3, as well as many other places. The King James refers to them as carnal. That word seems a bit harsh to us today—babes is a more caring description.

b. Maturing Christians. These can be found in many places. One rather instructive and wide-ranging list is in the Seven Letters to the Churches—in Revelation (chapters two and three). Jesus compliments their good qualities, and warns them of their need to overcome bad characteristics. Failure here is to risk missing Heaven.

c. Mature Christians. These are mentioned by Paul in 1st Corinthians 2:6, and indirectly at other places such as Philippians 4:9 and Colossians 1:28. The KJV refers to them as perfect. Perfect seems impossible to us today, because of its connotation. The New International Version has chosen a better word by stating, "mature."

3. "End Times" troubles will also have impact on the issues presented in this book. In Luke 23:31, Jesus said,

"For if men do these things when the tree is green, what will happen when it is dry?" (NIV)

He was being crucified on a wooden cross. Every century since then has allowed that wood to become more and more dry. Every century since then has seen mankind more able and more likely to do more harm to his fellow man.

Divorce is just one of many areas where mankind is farther and farther from the will of God. One major impact here is for the "innocent," or relatively innocent, spouses who are stuck in a hateful marriage. Would God have us fail to offer them His rescue?

Yes, we lament the rising divorce rates. Yes, we try to slow this rise. But when we try too hard, we do more damage than good. Statistics abound about the rise of divorce but where are the statistics about psychological abuse? They are much more difficult to measure, and are therefore lost in the dust & commotion about the so-called sin of divorce. Actually divorce may or may not be sin—for some it is—and for others, it is not.

As wickedness increases, righteousness must also increase. Such polarization is a mark of the end times. As unnecessary "putting away" (and divorce) increases, rescues must also increase. The desire to see such rescues handled Biblically—creates a burden. This burden is the primary reason for this book about *"Divorce as 'Required' by Scripture."* Life is moving faster than at any other time in history. Good Christians must be "up to speed" with the rescue of hurting and broken spouses.... Here lies one of the largest "mission fields" in America.

4. False guilt and assignment as second class Christian, are too often put upon victims of unwanted and undeserved divorce. On the other hand, this does not mean that guilt and shunning are out of place for those whose hardheartedness leads to divorce. It's just the blanket prejudice against divorce that needs to be stopped. This is true not only for its victims but also for the victimizers. Victimizers already risk missing Heaven. Their lack of mercy will lead to a lack of mercy for themselves on judgment day—unless forgiveness is found before then. So, why not help them too?

Church people should be looking more closely at how and why a believer, or un-believer, got divorced. In those cases where divorce was for honorable reasons, church folks should be the first to pray for, and welcome, 100-fold solutions. This was addressed in chapter six.

Deserved guilt should also be addressed briefly. It should be punished—thru Godly discipline. It should also be forgotten—unless & until its root would again be seen. Deserved guilt is likely to interfere with any chance at a 100-fold solution until one has thoroughly repented of it. Such repentance is also likely to include a related period of penance.

5. Rapture readiness was mentioned in the introduction of this book. This writer still believes in that catching up of prepared believers to meet the Lord Jesus Christ in the clouds. See 1st Thessalonians 4:17 and 1st John 3:3. The latter verse talks about making oneself pure. The former shows that those who are prepared in Christ will meet Him in the air. Later on, He will put His foot down upon Mount Zion (Zechariah 14:4 and Revelation 14:1). That is when many other folks, who were not prepared, will see Him.

With apologies to those who do not see it this way, one more point should still be made. To be ready to meet Jesus in the clouds, or here on the earth, means to be pure. (See Titus 2:11-14, and again 1st John 3:3.) Otherwise, one is not ready. It seems to me that the unmerciful are not pure. Even worse are those who are knowingly and willingly unmerciful. How can they expect the Lord's best? How can they expect to be called up to meet Him in the air?

Many traditionalists in the church are unmerciful about divorce (and remarriage). They should take another look at the need to properly rescue the many victims mentioned in this book. They will need to give up the black-or-white solution, in favor of a broader, kingdom-building solution. If they fail to do this they may miss God's best in regard to being raptured. But He, in His great mercy may rapture them anyway. This writer would suggest that "earning" God's best—like His upcoming rapture—will likely include proper treatment of those who have been unnecessarily "put away." The same applies for many victims of divorce.

6. <u>Poll analysis</u> can, and often does, sway opinions. It is true that divorce often has tragic effects on children. The polls, as well as scientific study, have proved this. One longs for similar polls and scientific studies to look at the other side of the coin. What about children whose dads ruin the image of fatherhood? What about children whose mothers have traded lovers somewhat like Israel traded in idolatry? Who can even identify these tragedies? What wicked and lasting effects have these kind of parents had on their children? After we begin to try to answer these questions, we may begin to have a good balance for how to handle broken marriages.

7. <u>Discernment</u> in handling damaged or broken marriages, can usually be helped with one basic question? There is of course a great need for honesty in answering it. The question for each spouse to ask of himself, and to be asked by a counselor, is simple but telling. It is this, "In all of the time that you have been married—have you ever given up on your marriage commitment?" Similarly—have you ever done anything to destroy your marriage relationship?

Then there are two deeper levels of this basic question. First is the issue of how frequently has one given up, or tried to destroy.... Second is the question of how intense or powerful was the act of giving up, or destroying. These steps of examination offer a very good and very simple way to discern what is at the heart of any marriage.

Spouses who know their marriage is in trouble, and who want to try and fix it, can ask themselves these same questions. The strength of their desire to fix it will be seen in how tenderly and lovingly they handle these deep issues of the heart. Either spouse should soon be able to tell whether the other spouse wants to completely repair the marriage. Obviously these matters will also need to be bathed in prayer. And then God will be able to tell how much either spouse wants to save the marriage.

8. Inductive Bible study is a highly valuable method of learning more about the word of God. It begins with asking the six English interrogatives: who? what? when? where? why? and how? After these results are compiled, conclusions can be drawn. These conclusions are usually less subjective than deductive study, and therefore much more valuable.

Deductive study is more open to me just looking for a verse to prove my point. The verse may prove my point but the larger context may disprove it. Taking a verse out of context is risky.

These methods have been raised for one special reason. The Triple-base solution used in this book has been based on a "Bible-wide" inductive study. Each of the three, Triple-base elements has been used in each area of the Bible where divorce appears to be required.

The Triple-base method is not just black-or-white, although the black-or-white method can be helpful on some issues. The black-or-white method would not find the word "divorce" in Exodus 21:1-6, and would therefore assume that divorce did not occur. The inductive study used as part of the Triple-base solution, does find divorce in that passage about Hebrew servants.

The servants in question came without a wife. The master gave them a wife. Children were born from their union. But the man often did not learn to love his job, wife, or kids. He was sent away. If that is not divorce, then what is?

One could easily conclude, that the black-or-white method is commonly used by new Christians, who have not matured in the word of God. One could also conclude that maturity in the word, requires that we let the word speak to us, about things that are obvious—even if unstated.

9. Bible Harmony can be described as: any pattern of a characteristic of God that repeatedly occurs from Genesis to Revelation. Such harmony includes His attributes, and doctrines recorded in His Word. This writer obviously believes that the doctrine (or teaching) about *"Divorce as 'Required' by Scripture"* is in very good tune with good Bible Harmony. Bible Harmony could also be described as the Bible-wide use of the Inductive Study Method. In any case, it should yield the fairest teaching possible on any thorny doctrine. Thorny as used here refers to going against tradition.

Traditionalists would also say that their support for the permanence of marriage can be proven with Bible Harmony. This writer would not disagree. My desire is for them to see that there is more than one viable doctrine in regard to marriage, and marriage breakdown. If they could but see this, then the thorn would disappear!

10. Remarriage is obviously related to divorce. Not much has been said about remarriage. This book has not been about remarriage. But some "bits" of advice seem worthwhile anyway.

a. remarriage is an obvious next step sometime after divorce. God did say that it is not good for man to live alone. Paul specifically recommended living the single life, and gave very spiritual reasons for it. On the other hand, Paul also made plenty of room for remarriage.

b. remarriage is the only way to make room for the reward of the 100-fold spouse, found in verses *29 and 30* of Matthew 19, and Mark 10, and Luke 18.

c. remarriage to a 100-fold spouse may require a number of years in the waiting stage…

d. remarriage to a 100-fold spouse would usually be worth it for the sake of the children. They get a 100-fold father or mother.

e. remarriage must be to a believer

f. remarriage is much more likely than celibacy. The Eleven apostles were about as close to Jesus as one could get. Yet Paul says that they all had wives. None is known to have been remarried—but none is known to have become a eunuch for the sake of the kingdom. Celibacy is apparently a very rare gift.

g. remarriage should not automatically disqualify a man from leadership in the church

h. remarriage must be preceded by genuinely "awesome " amounts of prayer

i. remarriage to a former wife (or husband) is forbidden by Deuteronomy 24:4. One major issue there was uncleanness. It has been removed for the church age, by Acts 10:28. On the other hand the issue of crucifying Christ a second time has not been removed (Hebrews 6:4-6). Therefore some remarriages to former spouses would be okay and some would not. A key issue here would be whether the first victim-spouse was knowingly and willfully "crucified" by a first victimizing-spouse.

11. Jesus recognized five marriages in John 4:18. Jesus did not say that the woman had had one husband and four adulterous relationships. He recognized marriage number one, marriage number two, marriage number three, marriage number four, and marriage number five. By this he also recognized four divorces. Two important points can be drawn from this verse.

a. if all marriages are made in Heaven, then Heaven must also recognize divorce....

b. if first marriages cannot be dissolved except thru natural death, then our Samaritan woman (above) must have married a bunch of old men—and waited for each one to die—before marrying again. This would be just one more silly deduction—a bit humorous too.

c. one un-provable issue also arises, i.e. did Jesus see this woman as a willful or knowing sinner? The answer is that we just do not know for certain. What we do know is this—Jesus chose her to be the first human to whom He made direct announcement of his Messiah-ship. What if she had been the innocent victim of five hardhearted husbands—each of whom had given her that bill of divorcement? Can you think of anyone more deserving of meeting the Messiah?

12. Single parenting is an invention of God. It is not his perfect will but he "permits" it—and even causes it, when necessary. He ordered it in Exodus 21:4, thru the expulsion of the unloving servant. It was single mothers back then—temporary, or otherwise. Today it is single mothers, or single fathers.

13. Male leadership. Bible Harmony methods show the word of God to be about 99-to-1 in favor of male leaders. Some would say that the ratio is actually 99.9-to-1. This matter is a whole book in itself. It is only mentioned here for its impact on the principle in Deuteronomy 24:1-4, as also addressed by the Pharisees and Jesus.

Jewish men were apparently allowed to "put away," or "send away" their wives along with a certificate of divorce. On the other hand the Bible does not give such allowance for Jewish women. This male priority of authority "harmonizes" with Genesis 3:16, 1st Corinthians 11:3, Ephesians 5:23, Colossians 3:18, 1st Timothy 2:12, 3:2 & 12, 1st Peter 3:1-6, etc. It is not my place to question why God made this harmonic pattern—He just did. But in regard to "putting away" and divorce, this pattern does lead into the New Testament, e.g. Jesus reference to the Deuteronomy passage, and Mark 10:12, which reads in the King James Version,

> "And if a woman shall put away her husband, and be married to another, she committeth adultery."

My note of interest here is that Mark was not writing of a new, "egalitarian" command by Jesus.... To the contrary, Mark was likely to have been recognizing the influence of the Roman world—which allowed a woman to remarry. Some of those women may not have gotten divorced before getting remarried. They would then have been adulterous—as indicated by Jesus.

One should also take note that in the Bible there are some rare exceptions to the principle of male leadership. A useful doctrine could be built upon these exceptions—if one keeps in mind that they are exceptions. One principle that helps build such a doctrine of exception to male leadership is that of men's failures. For example, Judge Deborah (Judges chapter 4) offered an easy victory to the man Barak. He was apparently a coward, and declined. The enemy fell at the hands of a woman.

This was not done to change the "perfect will" of God, in regard to male leadership. It was done to shame Barak for his lack of leadership. God was at work within His "permissive will." The same thing often applies to broken marriages.

When a husband is not being a good leader, he can expect God to bless his wife with the exercise of good leadership. Also, especially today, when men are so often so hardhearted —women seem to be blessed by God with unusual leadership abilities. (And this includes the responsibility to initiate divorce when necessary.)

Having said this, one must also be wary of misuse of such "leadership." Women need to be sure that they are within Bible models when they take such action. This book puts forward several teachings about how to have assurance that one is taking Biblical action. Such assurances should encourage long-suffering victims of ungodly marriages to end such marriages. They can do this with faith that the Heavenly Father is delivering them even as a good earthly father would.

Here again one thinks especially of the Jewish woman, or the Christian fundamentalist. Usually neither of them seems able to initiate a divorce—murder maybe—but divorce, never! Please pardon attempt at humor, but it is useful to dramatize the great need for reform. One wishes for some humor in other places in this book but efficiency seemed to preclude it. Now, that we are in the last chapter, why not?

Bits "Buffet" (second trip, continue counting)

14. Prayer & Fasting, and waiting on the good LORD. It seemed needful for a respite after finishing the first draft of this book about *"Divorce as 'Required' by Scripture."* During this respite of over a year, plenty of fervent prayer, and a variety of fastings, were applied in hopes of hearing more from the good LORD. He did not disappoint me. I felt the need for more reinforcement

about the difference between "apoluo" (put away) and "apostasion" (divorce). This need was especially strong for two reasons: first, in regard to the small chance of being totally wrong and therefore misleading any number of folks; and second, in regard to what my opponents are likely to need in helping them change their minds. Plenty of reinforcement arrived. It was also good to let the book "simmer" awhile on the back burner and then take a fresh look at it. However, my burden to get it out into the hands of those who might use it did increase. May God forgive me if the wait was not worth the reinforcements that have arrived. They will be listed first and then some other "bits" will be added to this chapter.

15. *Women in Chains, A Sourcebook on the Agunah*, edited by Jack Nusan Porter; published in 1995 by Jason Aaronson Inc., Northvale, NJ has become my greatest reinforcement. (One could wish that it had been discovered sooner.) Dr. Porter has an earned Ph.D. from Northwestern University and is well acquainted with the Jewish community. He has compiled a well-balanced book about the agunah problem within the Jewish religion—both here and in Israel. Agunah is the word applied to a Jewish woman who is separated (or divorced by civil court) from her husband but who is not able to remarry. She cannot remarry until she receives a certificate of divorce from her husband—as described in chapter 3, '*Converted by Callison.*'

We now have not just Walter Callison's research but an entire book about this important issue. It is not my purpose here to give a book report—but simply to import the weight of Porter's book on the issue of the "put away" woman. Porter does not deal with the Hebrew grammar but he nevertheless paints an exact picture of what this writer has come to see as the "put away" woman.

The agunah problem can be further investigated online with hundreds of hits—using just the word agunah, or agunot. Newspaper articles, court cases and support groups are listed with recurring similarities. Some examples are: an article in the *Jewish Encyclopedia* by David Werner Amram; articles in various newspapers quoting *The Jerusalem Report,* an article by the *Baltimore Jewish Times,* others by *The New York Jewish Week* and the *Cleveland Jewish Times;* also in the *University of Louisville Journal of Family Law,* the *Illinois Bar Journal, Berkeley Women's Law Journal,* and the *Harvard Women's Law Journal;* court cases reported in the *Journal of Law and Religion,* and the *Jewish Law Annual;* a Maryland Attorney General's ruling, an appellate case in the New York State Supreme Court....

The weight of this contemporary evidence can hardly be overstated. It even brought a brilliant pastor friend to agree that by extrapolation we can likely prove the "put away" woman existed since the time of Moses. Consider Ecclesiastes 1:9, and then 3:15(a) below:

> 9 What has been will be again,
> what has been done will be done again;
> there is nothing new under the sun. NIV
>
> 15(a) Whatever is has already been,
> and what will be has been before; NIV

In other words, if Jewish men are "putting away" their wives today, then they were doing it in the time of Moses. And if they were doing it in the time when Moses wrote Deuteronomy 24:1-4, then they will be doing it today.

P.S. The weight of this agunah evidence is causing the conservative, middle-aged pastor friend to reconsider his whole approach to divorce and remarriage.... This again shows that the Jewish perspective needs to be considered on almost every religious issue—Old Testament, and New Testament.

16. Retraction by Dr. William A. Heth published in *The Southern Baptist Journal of Theology* (Spring 2002, Vol. 6, No. 1). This reinforcement carries almost as much weight as the book by Dr. Porter about the agunah. There are a number of reasons for this retraction to have such high impact, including: (a) Dr. Heth first wrote, with Gordon J. Wenham, in 1984 of their strong oppositions to divorce and remarriage, (b) in 1997, these two scholars published a second edition of their book *Jesus and Divorce* by Thomas Nelson, (c) the three "years" above show almost two decades of strong opinion being changed by an older (and now wiser) professor, (d) Heth was at the famous Dallas Theological Seminary when the book was first published; Wenham was at the College of St. Paul and St. Mary in Cheltenham, England, (e) despite co-author Wenham's not having changed his mind, Heth makes lengthy explanation of how and why he has changed his mind, (f) one especially telling portion of Heth's recant in the SBJT is about the pastoral implications (page 20). Here he writes of finding increased cause to see that Jesus would not forbid remarriage to an "innocent person whose

spouse's unrepentant sexual immorality or subsequent remarriage had made the resolution of the original marriage impossible," and (g) the *Jesus and Divorce* book by Heth & Wenham has given great impact to the position of no divorce, and no remarriage after divorce—and now that impact is significantly lessened.

Before leaving Heth & Wenham, one potentially huge flaw in their book should be mentioned. They relied heavily upon one source, i.e. Henri Crouzel's *L'eglise primitive face au divorce du premier au cinquieme siecle.* Paris: Beauchesne, 1971. Jesuit Crouzel is apparently French and therefore introduces the likelihood of additional translation difficulties. Crouzel would have been studying the Greek and/or Latin of the early church fathers and writing in French. Even if Heth & Wenham made their own translation of Crouzel, that would have added significant possibilities of error.

In addition to such language difficulties, one cannot help but wonder whether Crouzel even came close to addressing the "apoluo" vs. "apostasion" issue as discussed earlier in this book. If he did not, then his great work would be suspect. If he did discuss the "put away" vs. divorce issue, then why didn't Heth & Wenham dig deeply into it with their book, or recent articles? This writer is somewhat suspicious of Crouzel's work but that is as far as it has gone for now.

As we leave Heth & Wenham, an unusual reinforcement for my findings should be mentioned—as given by them. They "admit" that not everyone agrees with Henri Crouzel's conclusions on so many of the early church Fathers. Opponents to Crouzel's thinking say that the early church Fathers tended to be ascetic. Asceticism involves strict self-denials for the purpose of elevating, or deepening, one's religious experience. Asceticism has had its impact on many religions, including Christianity; sometimes for the good, and sometimes not. It seems to me that asceticism tendencies would have been quite likely to influence the early church Fathers—in forbidding divorce, and remarriage. It may be where "die for the cause" began. My problem, as mentioned earlier in this book, is that martyrdom should not be put upon others, and especially not with blanket application. It should be a choice—made by a smaller percentage of believers. Blanket statements about the so-called "sin of divorce," can and have pushed many spouses into martyrdom (figuratively, and literally).

17. Pastoral proofs are often "in the pudding." Pastors are out there where the rubber meets the road. They see first hand what works and what does not, and are not afraid to let the scholars know about it. Professor Heth is not the first professor, or highly educated person, to change his mind when faced with the pastoral application of an ivory tower doctrine—that just doesn't work. His former co-author Wenham stated in the same SBJT (page 43) that, "sometimes the church may with a heavy heart have to sanction divorce among its own members, and exceptionally as some bishops in Origen's day did, even tolerate remarriage 'to avoid worse evils.' " Dr. Wenham has not changed his written theology but has made a way to occasionally live with divorce and remarriage. This is likely due to the pastoral implications. On the other hand, Dr. Larry Richards wrote as a scholar but with a pastor's heart when he made room for divorce and

remarriage in his book *Remarriage, A Healing Gift from God.* Also on the other hand is Reverend Walter Callison whose heart of pastoral experience led him to write *Divorce, A Gift of God's Love* (as highlighted in chapter 3).

Erasmus and most of the Reformers noticed that their doctrine against divorce and remarriage was not working all that well, and found ways to get themselves out of that theological box. One method was to assume that a deserting spouse would commit adultery. Such adultery would have been punishable by death under the Law of Moses. Therefore the deserting spouse was considered figuratively "dead" before God, and the other spouse could remarry.

The Roman Catholic Church gets around the presumed beliefs of the early church Fathers by providing annulments. An "illegal" marriage, even of many years, can be annulled because God did not join them in the first place. (Illegal being defined as not within the will of God.) This writer thinks that God must be amused by most of the above mentioned efforts to uphold Jesus' supposed opposition to divorce—while at the same time allowing folks to do what Jesus (supposedly) said not to do. Why not just try a more logical translation of those two words "apoluo" and "apostasion?"

18. Saddle-up for Sleep "Syndrome" is a device made especially for this second trip to the salad bar of *'Book Closing Bits.'* This syndrome is devised as a poignant method of describing unexplainable, theological flip-flop. It will be used just now to draw attention to a pattern among many Bible commentators and scholars. Most of these fine Christian men accurately define the two

different words: "apoluo" (put away), and "apostasion" (divorce). However, they then ignore the difference, and even contradict it, by their written comments about how Jesus supposedly opposed divorce.... It seems that "tradition" has them so deeply brainwashed that they automatically put their logic to sleep—as soon as they get past the basic definitions of the two words in question.

In two upcoming areas (#19 and #21), one could write a long chapter about this "Saddle-up for Sleep Syndrome." However, time and space do not permit, and the reader is probably not all that interested anyway. Therefore within each area only one or two sources will be expanded to specifically show the "Saddle-up for Sleep Syndrome." This flip-flop exposure is not meant to be negative in any personal way. In fact some would say that church tradition is simply having its proper place in their writings. This writer wishes that they would properly explain their departure from their own definitions—if such explanation would even be viable.

19. Commentary "support" is next on my list. A number of commentaries show definite wording that strongly supports the difference between "apoluo" and "apostasion." A related weakness is that they do not follow through that well with applying the difference. They commonly show the "Saddle-up for Sleep Syndrome." Their works are listed, with underlining supplied, primarily to strengthen the proof of those two words having different meanings. It seems to this writer that they are somewhat like Erasmus and many Reformers. They know what the words mean but do not

seem able to apply them in a straightforward way—due to the pressure of many centuries of church tradition.

Rex Mason on *The Books of Haggai, Zechariah, and Malachi* states (page 150) in regard to Malachi 2:13-16 that the text did not originally condemn divorce. Divorce had never been prohibited by Judaism. "A man could not simply put his wife away. He had to write a bill of divorce...." Mason is apparently therefore saying that Malachi does not report on a God who hates divorce. That leaves us with a God who hates "putting away."

C.E.B. Cranfield on *The Gospel According to Saint Mark* states (page 319) that apostasion in the Greek is the equivalent of keriythuwth in the Hebrew—as shown by the Septuagint. Both words mean divorce.

Eugene LaVerdiere on *The Beginning of the Gospel: introducing the Gospel according to Mark* states (page 67) that Moses permitted the husband to write a bill of divorce (biblion apostasiou) and dismiss (apolysai) her. Notice again the two distinctly different words—one for divorce and the other for dismissal or "sending away."

Robert G. Bratcher and Eugene Albert Nida in *A Translator's Handbook on the Gospel of Mark* state (page 309) that the word "apostasion" (putting away) is always used by the Septuagint in the sense of divorce; and further that "biblion apostasiou" means a document of divorce, or a certificate of divorce.

An expansion to show the "Saddle-up for Sleep Syndrome" is now included. Near the bottom of that same page 309, one finds this explanation, "*Put her away* must not be translated literally in most languages, for this would imply 'storing her' or 'placing her in a position away from people', a not uncommon mistake in translating." It seems to me that this is not a mistake, but is in fact an accurate rendering. The agunah of today is "stored," even "figuratively caged," away from any chance at a second marriage.

20. Septuagint sightings are a direct reinforcement to a correct translation of apostasion. Did you notice two sightings within the preceding section 19? C.E.B. Cranfield's commentary on Mark states that apostasion in the Greek is the equivalent of keriythuwth in the Hebrew, as shown by the Septuagint. Bratcher and Nida, on Mark, use the word "always" in regard to apostasion meaning divorce in the Septuagint. They further state that "biblion apostasiou" means a document of divorce, or a certificate of divorce, in the Septuagint.

So what is the need to emphasize the Septuagint? It is supportive of the word definitions preferred in this book about divorces. The Septuagint has the Old Testament translated into Greek. This work was completed in the third century before Christ. It shows the Greek equivalent to the Hebrew words. This is especially helpful in regard to the words used by Jesus. It shows the King James Version and the Wuest Translation to be accurate, and modern translations to be inaccurate. Jesus was not saying the word for divorce, when he "said" apoluo. The word for divorce is apostasion. Apoluo therefore must only mean "put away." Putting away may, or may not, have included divorce papers....

There are direct Septuagint works that also support these uses of apostasion—to mean divorce. These other works also support the idea that God hates "putting away," and does not hate divorce, e.g. the Hatch & Redpath Concordance (page 489, center column). He especially would not hate divorce when it made necessary rescue of a victim wife—from an ungodly marriage.

In Malachi 2:16, the Septuagint uses Strong's #1821. It is transliterated into English by the word exapostello. This word means to send away. Strong's does not even mention divorce as an afterthought for this word; neither does Thayer's Lexicon. One wonders whether the translators of modern Bibles checked the Septuagint. There are many other reinforcements from the Septuagint but there is no need to spread them out here. The Septuagint evidence seems almost overwhelming—in its support for the word definitions preferred in this book about divorce being required by Scripture.

21. <u>Exegetical & Theological Dictionaries</u> also show support for the sharp difference between divorce and "put away," and again <u>underlining is supplied</u>. On the other hand they too fail, like the commentaries, to follow through with applying those differences. It seems that the "Saddle-up for Sleep Syndrome" is epidemic.

This writer continues to believe that where there is smoke there is fire but that it has been invisible and ignored due to the billowing smoke of centuries-old church tradition. This writer is not against tradition in general—but is against tradition that is not properly attached to Scripture. This writer would ask the question, how can a word be defined as one thing and then applied as something significantly different?

The *Exegetical Dictionary of the New Testament* with editors Balz and Schneider, Volume 1, page 140 lists "apoluo" as set free, release; dismiss. In the 13 Synoptic occurrences, "apoluo" is a common term "for the dismissal of a woman from marriage by means of a letter of divorce (apostasion)," as in send away a wife.

Page 141 gives a separate listing for apostasion (transliterated from the Greek, as before) with a meaning of certificate of divorce. We again see two distinctly different words, and meanings.

A Dictionary of Early Christian Beliefs, with editor David W. Bercot does not directly address "apoluo" and "apostasion" but does give some interesting information under the following entries. Letters "a" and "b" refer to left and right columns, respectively.

DIVORCE
page 219b, 2nd entry attributed to Origen. Dissolution of marriage is used interchangeably with "put away a wife." The divorce allowance for the cause of fornication is in view. Origen wonders whether poisoning would not also be an allowance that Jesus would make. However he then labels this as impious.

MONTANISTS
page 463b, C. No second marriages, viewpoint attributed to Tertullian. If a spouse dies, remarriage is against the will of God—for if He had wanted the marriage state to

continue, He would not have allowed the one spouse to die. Montanists excommunicated those who were twice married—after becoming believers. (page 464a)

REMARRIAGE
page 554b, entry attributed to Athenagoras. Second marriages, even after the death of a spouse, are adultery....

TWICE-MARRIED
page 658a, fourth entry attributed to 'Apostolic Constitutions.' A man twice married, after baptism, cannot be a bishop, presbyter, or deacon.

The New International Dictionary of New Testament Theology with General Editor Colin Brown, Vol I: A-F, page 21 lists Divorce with the transliterated Greek word "apostasion." The main entry is on pages 505. Again here the word apostasion is listed as "divorce," and the word apoluo is listed as "to set free" (or send away, or put away).

The "Saddle-up for Sleep Syndrome." enters at the bottom of page 505. Apoluo is shown as release of a prisoner (Mk 15:6-15), release of a debtor (Mt 18:27), set free from disease (Lk 13:12), to send away people (Mk 6:36, 45; 8:3, 9), etc. However when one turns the page, he finds apoluo suddenly changes in meaning, with regard to a wife, and now means divorce (Mt 1:19, 5:31f., 19:3, 7-9; Mk. 10:2, 4, 11f.; Lk. 16:18). Apostasion gets honorable mention as divorce for Mt 5:31, 19:7, and Mk 10:4.

Notice that Mt 5:31, 19:7 and Mk 10:4 are on both lists—and both supposedly mean divorce. However in the Greek text two different words are used in each of these verses, i.e. "apoluo" and "apostastion." How can they mean the same thing?

This "blows" my mind—mainly because it is done without any good explanation, but also because of the unexplained flip-flop in translation. The flip-flop does fit nicely with the rest of page 506, e.g. a man who divorces his wife and remarries is committing adultery. Tradition has again usurped logic!

A Dictionary of the Bible by John D. Davis, Ph.D, D.D., page 172 lists Divorce, Divorcement. Under Moses the process of divorce included two things: first, the husband presented the bill of divorce to his wife; and second, he sent her away. This is reinforcing for the premise of divorce being different from put away. However, Davis goes on to say that a man who puts his wife away..., and remarries—commits adultery. He has lost sight of the need for the two steps he just described. He does not even address the two-step process for church age people.

The *Expository Dictionary of Bible Words* by Lawrence O. Richards is given attention for at least two reasons. First is his method of making "definitions." On Preface pages *ix* and *x*, he explains the need to consider original languages, and another need, i.e. to consider how such words are used to build a "biblical concept." The writer of *"Divorce as 'Required' by Scripture"* was taught the strength of this method in the mid 1980's—about the same time that Richards was writing his dictionary. This method is the primary technique used within my book.

Secondly, and with some disappointment, Richards addresses Divorce and Remarriage (page 232-235). He is traditional in his biblical concept of these terms; however, he is not harsh. He does not address the Greek words "apoluo" and "apostasion." In his conclusion, he becomes rather pastoral and non-judgmental. He further states that the church must not legislate divorce or remarriage.

The New Unger Bible Dictionary by Merrill F. Unger, page 314 lists Divorce—with a parenthetical that shows the Hebrew "keriythuwth" to equal the Greek "apostasion." Here is some further support for the pattern shown earlier in this book between Old Testament and New Testament word choices for divorce. On the other hand, Unger has taken up with the traditionalists in various New Testament applications, e.g. "he who marries a divorced woman commits adultery." It seems to me that he who marries a "put away" woman is the one who commits adultery.

The *New International Dictionary of Old Testament Theology and Exegesis* by William A. VanGemeren is now considered for a number of reasons. First VanGemeren adds a new Hebrew word for "drive out," or "put away," i.e. garash (Strong's #1644; VanGemeren #1763, Volume 1, page 898). It can also mean cast out/divorce a wife. Secondly, in Volume 2, page 718 VanGemeren lists keriythuwth with its usual Hebrew meaning of divorce. In his comments he too reinforces the two separate steps in regard to Deuteronomy 24:1, i.e. writing the certificate of divorce for placement into her hand, and sending her out of his house. Thirdly, in Volume 4, pages 119 to 123 he discusses "shalach" with a meaning of send away. At the bottom of page 120 is mention of shalach being used in the context of divorce (but not as a substitute word for divorce). On page 122 one discovers some strong reinforcement for the statement that God hates "putting away," and not divorce. VanGemeren aptly draws attention to the difficult text of Malachi 2:16. He says that the "traditional" rendering (I hate divorce) is impossible! One strong proof of this is the use of a variation of shalach in Exodus 18:2 where Moses is "sending away" his wife Zipporah. Did God hate Moses for that? This writer would say no way.

An Expository Dictionary of New Testament Words by W. E. Vine, M.A. lists the verb "apoluo" in three locations: with the word "put," with the word "dismiss (-ed)," and with the word "divorce," (or divorcement). On this last entry, he also includes "apostastion," but as a noun. He allows enough overlap to deduct that he did not dig deeply into this one.

The Complete Word Study Dictionary: New Testament by Spiros Zodhiates, Th.D. gives perhaps the most reinforcement to the case made in this book about the difference between "apoluo" (put away) and "apostasion (divorce)." His broad, general treatment is on pages 233, and 236-37. His uniqueness is on the issue of the "certificate of innocence," that is, his equivalent for the certificate of divorce. A man who would marry a woman when she did not have this "certificate of innocence," would have "adultery committed against himself." He also makes fair usage of the term "innocent spouse." He allows apostasion to include departure, dismissal, or divorce. However, he applies apostasion to the actual deed or instrument of divorce. His issue with innocence is a good lead into the next section.

22. The Hammurabi Code of ancient Babylon is famous for its "fairness," in those times—about seventeen centuries before Christ. It is helpful to the case made in this book about the difference between the dismissal of a wife, and the certificate used to dismiss her. The Code of Hammurabi and the Law of Moses have a significant number of similarities. One apparent difference is in regard to adultery. For Moses it was a moral issue—punishable by death. For Hamurrabi "ordinary" adultery was apparently not punishable by death.... Neither did the dismissal of an ordinary wife require a certificate of divorce. A verbal dismissal was sufficient. If a formalized marriage was to be dissolved, courts sometimes got involved....

The bottom line for this writer is that Moses had to require the certificate of divorce—in order to protect the dismissed, or sent away, wife. Without this "walking paper," the sent away woman could later be charged with adultery—and stoned to death. This would be especially true if her (former) husband would purposely "forget" his spoken dismissal. He would then effectively have murdered his wife—perhaps without even having to help throw the stones.

God made adultery punishable by death and God therefore provided a protection for the dismissed, sent away, or put away woman. The poignant issue is that there were two separate actions: (a) *writing* a certificate of divorce, and (b) *sending* away. Therefore Moses used two different words. More importantly to us, two different words were recognized by Jesus Christ. In Mark 10:5, He referred to the twin concept as part of a precept (KJV), or law (NIV), of Moses. These "twins" have the same root ("apo"), but these are not identical twins. The words "apoluo" and "apostasion" cannot be safely interchanged; neither can "shalach" and (sefer) "keriythuwth."

23. Garash, Strong's #1644, is the transliterated Hebrew word which means: to expel...to drive out. Gesenius' Lexicon, page 181 specifically mentions to "put away," to divorce a wife. It then lists five Scriptures where a "wife" is part of the story. This writer would add a sixth (Gen 21:10). There is the story of Hagar, Abraham's concubine who was sent away by him. His wife Sarah had wanted Hagar to be expelled. Sarah used Hebrew word #1644. In Genesis 21:14, Abraham's actual sending away of Hagar is recorded as Hebrew word #7971—shalach. These two words can be used interchangeably. One interesting point, for this writer, is that no certificate of divorce is mentioned with either word. The Hebrew word shalach stands alone as a "putting away," or sending away. This seems to further support one of the major premises of this book, i.e. that shalach does not mean the same thing as keriythuwth. (See also Genesis 25:6 in regard to sending away, #7971; and Judges 11:2 in regard to being expelled.)

It also seems to me that Gesenius has taken up with the traditionalists. Why else would he assign two meanings to the one word garash? Such assignment is convenient but is it accurate? If it did not mean divorce in Genesis 21, then why might it mean divorce elsewhere in Leviticus and Numbers? Moses wrote the first five books of the Bible. When Moses wrote about divorce, he used keriythuwth (Dt 24:1-4).

Gesenius' five Scripture references are: Leviticus 21:7, 14; 22:13; Numbers 30:10 (sic) but see verse 9; and Ezekiel 44:22. In each of these Scriptures, this writer concludes that "put away" is the more likely and more accurate meaning of what was being reported. Therefore, there is no need for Gesenius to include the word divorce, unless he would explain it as a related, additional issue.

24. Overlapping definitions occur in any number of places in the Bible. Whole chapters could be written on each of these but time and space do not permit. Several are mentioned here to show that the term "put away" and the word "divorce" are not so unusual in this regard.

Jesus had many disciples but only twelve were named as apostles. Apostle is Strong's #652—apostolos, and disciple is Strong's #3101—methetes. Sometimes these words overlap and sometimes they do not, e.g. Matthew 10:1-2.

Fasting is sometimes "omitted" by the NIV, when the King James includes it. Some folks would say that the KJV added it and the NIV footnote is more proper. My point is that prayer and fasting are somewhat overlapped. When one is mentioned, the other may be presumed. But even this presumption does not always apply. See Luke 5:33-35. An aside here is a mention of the "King James Only" crowd. They seldom trust any modern translation. There is a good book written by James R. White, which exposes much unfair treatment of modern translations. It is listed in the bibliography.

Wine denotes fermentation, but in the Greek it can also be translated as unfermented (grape juice). The Greek word for fermented wine is oinos—Strong's #3631, as used in Mark 15:23. Back in Mark 14:23, the cup is mentioned in regard to communion. Two major denominations use fermented juice at their communion services. Their "cup" of grape juice, or fruit of the vine, is fermented—but the communion Scriptures do not support this application. We again see overlap—especially in the application of the text. Jack Van Impe has written a fine book about the differences, the errors and the impossibility of the fermentation of concentrated grape juice (also thought of as grape honey). His book is listed in the bibliography.

Rahab is known as a harlot—but she made it into the genealogy of Jesus (Mt. 1:5). The great commentator Adam Clarke makes a strong case that Rahab does not need to be seen as a harlot. The Hebrew word in question is zanah, Strong's #2181. This word can also mean innkeeper, or tavern-keeper. There is room for overlap in between prostitute and female tavern-keeper in many societies, but this fact alone does not prove that Rahab was a harlot. Perhaps she once was a harlot and an innkeeper—who then gave up harlotry, and just kept the inn.... My point is that we again have language overlap, and cannot be absolutely sure about Rahab's condition(s).

Bits "Buffet" (dessert trip, continue counting)

25. "As iron sharpens iron, so one man sharpens another," is found in Proverbs 27:17 (NIV); underlining supplied. About a half dozen cases are now given to show this phenomenon. Each begins with two arrows (>>). These cases are supposed to be like the icing on the cake. They are some of my strongest proofs about iron-sharp theology and its impact upon this book.

>>Jeremiah 18:7-10 seems to this writer to so sharpen Numbers 23:19 that it actually *trumps* it. The Numbers verse says that God is not a man that He should...change His mind, but the Jeremiah passage seems to *override* that verse in Numbers. The Jeremiah verses read as follows:

> "7 If at any time I announce that a nation or kingdom is to be uprooted, torn down and destroyed, 8 and if that nation I warned repents of its evil, then I will relent and not inflict on it the disaster I had planned. 9 And if at another time I announce that a nation or kingdom is to be built up and planted, 10 and if it does evil in my sight and does not obey me, then I will reconsider the good I had intended to do for it." NIV

In Numbers 23, Balaam was speaking to Balak about the nation of Israel as a whole—over a long period of time. In Jeremiah, the address is about the ups and downs during that long period of time.

>>"Who killed Jesus? " has become a popular question in our time due, in part, to the movie by Mel Gibson—*The Passion of the Christ.* Folks who are into the sovereignty of God often go to Isaiah 53:10 to show the

general truth that it was the Lord's will to crush His son Jesus. Some are so bold as to say that "God killed Jesus." This writer finds to the contrary in 1st Thessalonians 2:14-16 which reads, with underlining supplied:

> "For you, brothers, became imitators of God's churches in Judea, which are in Christ Jesus: You suffered from your own countrymen the same things those churches suffered from the Jews, 15 who killed the Lord Jesus and the prophets and also drove us out. They displease God and are hostile to all men 16 in their effort to keep us from speaking to the Gentiles so that they may be saved. In this way they always heap up their sins to the limit. The wrath of God has come upon them at last." NIV

The underlined is much more specific, and weighty than that generalization from Isaiah 53. This underlined portion is further solidified by Jesus own words in John 10:17-18 which reads with underlining supplied:

> "The reason my Father loves me is that I lay down my life—only to take it up again. 18 No one takes it from me, but I lay it down of my own accord. I have authority to lay it down and authority to take it up again. This command I received from my Father." NIV

Even within the quote, there is an occasion for iron to sharpen iron. The word "command" in the last sentence might be spun toward the sovereignty of God. However, in the Greek it can mean precept, or authority. The context sharpens the meaning to give yet further support to the conclusion that Jesus had the power (authority) to choose to let the Jews kill Him. God allowed…even recommended...it, but Jesus chose it, and the Jews did it. Please note that this does not make me anti-Semitic; to the contrary, it makes me want to be more like Jesus. Also worth noting here is the kind help given to me from the Jewish community—during the research of this book.

>>Paul and Jesus were single men during their ministry. They both recommended celibacy, for those who were able to accomplish it. They seem to have *trumped* the Old Testament edict to be fruitful and multiply. One can *trump* this Old (& New) Testament principle by noting that Paul and Jesus were fruitful—but not in the biological sense. Their fruit was in regard to new babes in Christ, born of the water and of the Spirit. Here again iron sharpens irons and shows the need to take a Bible-wide view of the matter in question.

>>Submission one to another is recommended to all Christians in Ephesians 5:21. Many preachers today use popular theology to say that this applies to the passage just after the verse. This means that husbands and wives should submit to each other. But this writer would sharpen that iron with some stronger, contextual iron from the exact same passage. Do Jesus and the church submit mutually to each other? The answer is obviously not. The context compares Jesus and the church to the husband and the wife; so, how can the popular theology come out like it does? Further support against the pop-theology is found in the very next chapter of Ephesians. There we find children & parents, and slaves & masters. This writer would ask the popular theologians: are children & parents supposed to be

mutually submissive? And: are slaves & masters to be mutually submissive? The sharper, and contextual, iron here would again say obviously not.

>>Jesus gave a "new" command in John 13:34-35. It reads as follows:

> "A new command I give you: Love one another. As I have loved you, so you must love one another. 35 By this all men will know that you are my disciples, if you love one another." NIV

"Love one another," is not a new command, in the sense used by Jesus. The Eleven apostles were closer than neighbors. Leviticus 19:18 told the Jews to love their neighbors as themselves. Therefore, this three-word command would not have been new to the Eleven. The new part was the next five words. Thus, with iron sharpening iron, the NIV should read, *"A new command I give you: Love one another as I have loved you."*

>>Lastly from the Bible is an example from Moses. In Deuteronomy 31:6 he told the Israelites that God would never leave them nor forsake them. Moses was strong like *iron* but God's *iron*-like strength sharpened Moses in verses 16 & 17 of the very same chapter. Therein God told Moses of how the Israelites would forsake Him, and that He would then forsake them. *Iron sharpens iron.*

Last in this section is an example from our times. Bob Pierce was the founder of Samaritan's Purse. Franklin Graham and Jeanette Lockerbie wrote a book about Bob's public ministry with the subtitle *This One Thing I Do.* It was quite a tribute to Bob. Many years later

Bob's daughter, Marilee Dunker, wrote a book to sharpen the story about her dad from the perspective of an insider's view of the family. Her book is entitled *Days of Glory, Seasons of the Night*. As the title suggests, things were not always so well done around home. In fact, she indicates that Bob's marriage was in shambles more than once. Iron sharpens iron....

So what is my main reason for this section? It is to show that Bible theology, as well as human biography, can often be sharpened when strong iron is applied. This writer believes that this book about *Divorce as 'Required' by Scripture* is the strong iron that is needed to sharpen many centuries of incomplete theology about divorce and remarriage. The preceding "sharpenings" were used to loosen up the reader's mind to the possibility that centuries of tradition sometimes need to be overturned.

One of the strongest rules of interpreting Scripture says that when the plain sense makes good sense, one should not make any other sense (of a text). It seems to me that the plain sense of apoluo ("put away") and apostasion (divorce) make the best sense in all their applications—as shown earlier, in chapter 9. Of course the same thing applies to shalach ("put away") and other words that mean the same thing, as opposed to the word keriythuwth (divorce), in the Old Testament.

A noteworthy help in making good sense is that specific texts should normally be given more weight than general texts, as long as the same issue is in view. Therefore the more specific texts override the general texts—as this writer has tried to demonstrate in the above examples. If three or more specific texts seem to be showing a "new" doctrine, then what we actually have is a lost, or undiscovered doctrine.

Such "new" doctrine may sometimes exist peacefully alongside generally known doctrines. At other times, the "new" doctrine must be allowed to override general doctrine(s). And sometimes the "new" doctrine must be used with very specific application, even as an exception to the general doctrine. This all leads to the next point—about hardheartedness. When there is no ongoing hardheartedness, the "Garden of Eden" doctrine applies, i.e. permanence of marriage. But when the hearts of men and women grow hard, "new" or undiscovered doctrine must be used to rescue the victims. This is a strong point of my Bible-wide inductive methodology. It weighs the larger picture, along with its pertinent details!

26. Hardheartedness is the reason that Jesus gives for Moses having allowed, or commanded, divorce. Many church leaders over many centuries have tried to avoid this issue. It seems to this writer (and researcher) that they were trying to do something admirable. That is, they were trying to uphold marriage. They appealed to the high ideal of no continual hardheartedness. But they were not recognizing the real world—where much hardheartedness was, and still is, in place. Such hardheartedness can be attributed to both the husband and the wife—although the husband commonly seems more capable of such continuing coldness. My bottom line here is in regard to Jesus teaching about divorce.

Jesus did not do away with one jot or tittle or the law (Matthew 5:18). Therefore, He did not do away with Moses' provision for divorce and sending away, or "putting away." Hardheartedness exists today just as much, if not more, than it did in the time of Moses. This means that the need to allow (or cause) divorce, exists just as much now as it did in Moses' time.

Jesus also came to fulfill the law, or make it complete. For example, mental adultery has been added to the sin of fleshly adultery, and murder can now be done with the tongue (from a wicked and hateful heart). Note however that these "figurative" additions by Jesus did not do away with the literal acts of adultery and murder. In the same way, Jesus' appeal to the permanence of marriage did not do away with the need for its dissolution when hardheartedness has gone on for too long a period of time.

Making silly translations about the permanence of marriage does not solve the problem for victims of hardheartedness. (Victims here include the spouse and any children.) Silly translations just allow oppressors to continue to get away with their cruelty.

Divorce and "putting away" are just the symptoms of the deeper problem of hardheartedness. Church leaders need to admit this and face it head on. If the hardhearted one cannot be cured, then his (or her) victim must be offered a godly rescue. Church leaders, who will not face this, are much like the Pharisees of Jesus' time. They too are guilty of hardheartedness—hardheartedness toward the victims of those with hardhearted spouses.

27. Functional Divide is a term now used to describe a general line between families that succeed and families that fail. That is to say, (a) between marriages that last and marriages that fail—through divorce; or, (b)

functional families versus dysfunctional families—in regard to raising children; or, (c) inter-dependency as opposed to co-dependency—among family members.

This section is somewhat editorial in nature, but it is based upon many decades of observation and over twenty years of intermittent research. It seems to me that a "functional divide" is likely to be the primary, unrecognized reason for the centuries long existence of church tradition—in regard to the permanence of marriage. Church leaders, scholars, and writers were commonly more likely to have "successful" marriages. They therefore were less likely to understand, or have sufficient compassion for, people with unsuccessful marriages.

Higher-class people, as well as devoutly religious folk, have a tendency to be "scandalized" by the idea of divorce or remarriage. They tend to avoid it at all costs—even the cost of living out an otherwise dead marriage. After all, divorce and/or remarriage are not usually helpful in getting ahead in life. Moreover, the average "layperson" in the church would also be less likely to understand, or have sufficient compassion for, people with unsuccessful marriages.

One helpful comparison here is what is known today as the "digital divide." On the upper side of the digital divide are people who own calculators, cameras without film, cell phones that send e-mail, and computers. On the lower side of the digital divide are people who do not even know how to operate any of those "upper side" devices, and could not afford them if they did. Lower side people have little, or no say, about anything. Upper side people usually set the pace, make the rules, and take "good" advantage of most situations. This is a natural phenomenon and this writer believes that it has greatly impacted the church in regard to its traditional, hard-line stance against divorce and remarriage.

One last "editorial" comment here is about what some have seen as a deathblow to the church. In the fourth century after Christ, Roman Emperor Constantine got together with capable leaders of a growing movement known as the Church. He made a deal with them. It boiled down to this—all Christians were suddenly given Roman citizenship, and all Roman citizens were suddenly given church membership. These two entities then became institutionalized in support of each other. Many problems arose, including what to do about troubled marriages. True believers would have been able to work out their differences with the help of the Holy Spirit, or fellow believers. However, un-regenerated people would have to be "forced" into submission to the idea of the permanence of marriage. This writer believes that this social phenomenon further reinforced the centuries old error that put wrong words into Jesus' mouth—making Him the one who condemns divorce and remarriage. The Church, and the "state," wanted families to stay together. They therefore reinforced each other, and appear to have conspired, against the plain sense of what Jesus actually said. Some probably did this unwittingly and with good intent, but others should have known better—and some probably did know better. If only we could find some of the writings of the ones who knew better....

28. Martyrdom as a gift, is an unusual dessert item. Consider this reasoning. If martyrdom is the most

like Christ, and therefore the highest of all gifts (or offices), then it is likely to be the most rewarded in Heaven. This makes it a dessert item.

On the other hand, when underdog spouses are repeatedly "forced" back to abusive situations, their "overseers" risk being guilty of unwitting murder. Such murder may be figurative, or literal, but it is still murder. The overseers are probably just following tradition, in order to preserve a marriage. If only they could consider the "new," or undiscovered doctrine discussed at the end of the earlier item 25 (iron sharpens iron).

This issue of martyrdom was discussed earlier in this book, but it is mentioned here again—so that it will have its own "headline." Church leaders and members are then more likely not to miss this point.

If martyrdom is a rare gift (or office), then leaders have rarely been right in their blanket rule about the permanence of marriage. They would also likely have been right by accident. That is to say they would not have known that some of their "victims" were able to receive such a heavy-duty gift. Most of their other victims, who did not let their faith be shipwrecked—and lived out a dead marriage, are likely to have great reward in Heaven. In fact their reward is likely to be greater than that of those rules-righteous overseers. Moreover, some of those rules-righteous overseers may not even get into Heaven.

29. The United Bible Societies publishes a series of Handbooks for translators. These cover a majority of the books of the Old and New Testaments. They are listed here as a very special item due to the unusually helpful comments for, and translations of, Malachi 2:16.

Other commentaries have stated that this text is "troubled," but the United Bible Societies Old Testament goes considerably beyond that. In the area where God supposedly says that He hates divorce, the UBS offers some strong support for a different view. It states that the Hebrew words in question could be translated, "If someone hates, let him divorce" (his wife). Notice how well this fits with the issue of hardheartedness, and Deuteronomy 24:1-4.

The UBS also list others who have leaned in the direction of such a translation, i.e. the Hebrew Old Testament Textual Project, the Septuagint, the Vulgate, Luther, and the New English Bible. The NEB and the Revised English Bible state the following for Malachi 2:16,

> " If a man divorces or puts away his wife, says the LORD God of Israel, he overwhelms her with cruelty, says the LORD of Hosts."

Yet one more unusual translation is offered by the UBS, in regard to translation elements called Assertion, and Objection. After considering these deep elements, Malachi 2:16 could read,

> But you say, "The LORD God of Israel says, 'Let anyone who hates his wife divorce her.'" Yet such a person covers himself with violence [or, acts like a robber], says the LORD Almighty. So guard your spirits and do not be disloyal.

There are pros and cons to this reading but they are too lengthy to list here. But please notice the huge difference between most modern translations of Malachi 2:16 and any of the above translations. Those above may not be widely used but they add to the likelihood that God does not hate divorce. One can only wish that the respected UBS would soon bring its New Testament commentary, about divorce and "put away," into line with the Jewish prophet Malachi.

30. The Jewish perspective is the last point in this section. It was highlighted in item 15 (*Women in Chains*). It is mentioned under desserts because the church seems to need regular reminders that we Gentiles have been grafted into Israel, the root of our salvation (Romans 11:17-24).

Unfortunately, replacement theology has grown stronger in recent times. Misguided, replacement theologians think that the church has replaced Israel. This makes a mess of their doctrine of end times, and weakens other doctrines as well. It also encourages many pastors and teachers to continue their relative ignorance about God's chosen race.

Romans 1:16 says that the Gospel is for the Jew first, and then for the Gentile. This writer says that, in this same way, the words of Jesus about divorce, or "putting away," must be prioritized with a Jewish perspective. Then it will easily be seen that divorce refers to a certificate, a piece of paper written by the Jewish husband. It will also easily be seen that "putting away" is a separate act, a sending away of a wife. These two acts, on the part of the Jewish husband, lie at the very heart of the argument of this book! May God bless them to the heart of your understanding.

Epilogue

If Ecclesiastes 1:9 and 3:15 be true, then there is truly nothing new under the sun. What is...has already been, and what will be...is now. This means that if Jewish husbands of today are vengefully "putting away" their wives without a writ of divorcement, then they have been doing it for centuries and will continue to do it. Vengeance would include any of the following: (a) little or no justification, (b) a lengthy time of "putting away," even for the rest of her life, (c) the husband's taking of a second wife or concubine, (d) extortion against the first wife so as to gain full custody of children, or to obtain money, etc. Such hardheartedness is not limited to those who claim to live according to the Law of Moses. It also happens among those of us who claim to live according to the gospel of Jesus Christ. Obviously something must be wrong in regard to "putting away" a wife (or a husband).

If modern translations of Matthew 5:32 and Luke 16:18 be true, then anyone who marries a divorced woman commits adultery. Why don't our modern translations speak specifically about anyone who marries a divorced man? This writer is not "into equal rights," but does find something—in this divorce area—to be obviously wrong with our modern translations.

My burden about these matters is increased because today so many laypersons use those two texts, and other related texts, in wrongful ways. Scholars also use them in wrongful ways but they know of ways to escape the impact of such harsh usage. I would propose a helpful solution for followers of Moses, or Jesus.

It seems to me that if we would just take a "long view" at how the Heavenly Father and His Son act with their respective, betrothed wives, then we might get a good grip on how we should act. Husbands here should compare themselves to God, or Jesus Christ, and wives should compare themselves to Israel, or the Church. (cf. Ephesians 5:23).

God betrothed a small ethnic community of Jewish people to Himself. This betrothal has yet to be fully consummated. Those Jews who died in the faith are "with" God now but are not yet celebrating the intimacy of marriage in the New Jerusalem. (The same is true for Christians who have been betrothed to Jesus Christ).

During this betrothal period, God's people often went astray. God loved them deeply, and was longsuffering toward them. However, He did need to discipline them for their own good. God "put away" His chosen people in at least the following five ways, given in historical order. First, He basically "arranged" their enslavement to the Egyptians for about 400 years. Second, He caused them to go into captivity at Babylon (modern day Iraq) for 70 years. Third, He "put away" Israel and gave her a certificate of divorce. Fourth, He left them without any prophets, for about 500 years. Fifth, He dispersed them throughout the world for about 2000 years. We can "see" God sending His betrothed out of his Canaan-land house for 400 years, 70 years, and 2000 years. We can also "see" Him allowing His betrothed to stay in the Canaan-land house while He generally refused to talk with her for about 500 years. We also "see" what is today known as divorce.

Scriptures to support the above history are numberless. A few of note are: Deuteronomy chapters 6-8; Jeremiah 3:8, 16:15, 25:11; Hosea 6:2 (+2nd Peter 3:8); Acts 2:9-11, 13:16-20; and the Books of Jeremiah and Hosea, in general. God's betrothal period with His chosen people has lasted about 4,000 years. Over half of that time has been marred by His having to "put away" His betrothed. Less than half of that time has seen some glorious periods of joyful relationship.

But we have been talking about Israel as a nation. Individual Jewish persons had various experiences with God. Some Jews may have enjoyed good relations with God for most of their lives, while others may never have gotten to "know" Him. The same is true today in the

Church of Jesus Christ. Some "members" have a personal relationship with Jesus Christ while others only know about Jesus Christ.

Keystone verses from the New Testament include Ephesians 5:22-33. It is my belief that verse 21 should not be attached to verses 22-33 because of the immediate context in chapter six. That is to say that parents and children are *not* mutually submissive one to another. Neither are masters and servants. And within verses 22-33, Jesus is *not* mutually submissive to His church. He is the head—just like the parent, and the master. Verse 21 is therefore not in focus just now except in a minor way. It does contain the idea that both "sides" have some need of each other. However, this does *not* make them equal. The key verses are now given (with underlining supplied):

> 22 Wives, submit to your husbands as to the Lord. 23 For the husband is the head of the wife as Christ is the head of the church, his body, of which he is the Savior. 24 Now as the church submits to Christ, so also wives should submit to their husbands in everything.
>
> 25 Husbands, love your wives, just as Christ loved the church and gave himself up for her 26 to make her holy, cleansing her by the washing with water through the word, 27 and to present her to himself as a radiant church, without stain or wrinkle or any other blemish, but holy and blameless. 28 In this same way, husbands ought to love their wives as their own bodies. He who loves his wife loves himself. 29 After all, no one ever

> hated his own body, but he feeds and cares for it, just as Christ does the church— 30 for we are members of his body. 31 "For this reason a man will leave his father and mother and be united to his wife, and the two will become one flesh." 32 This is a profound mystery – but I am talking about Christ and the church. 33 However, each one of you also must love his wife as he loves himself, and the wife must respect her husband. NIV

The last words of Jesus to His church (bride-to-be) are found in Revelation chapters two and three. They are a bit too long to print here but several important principles are worth mentioning. *First* is the need to overcome. In all seven letters Jesus talked about the need of believers to overcome. *Second* is an exceptional church. Philadelphia alone was noted for little strength—yet this is the only church promised to be kept out of the great trial to come upon the whole earth. This church alone did not hear Jesus talk about anything He held against them. *Third* is a church that was (is) neither hot nor cold. Laodicea was told by Jesus that He was about to vomit them out of His body. They were in the body but needed to overcome lukewarmness—or be ejected.

Now with this "long view" of godly husbandry in mind, let's make some deductions—related to the issues within this book.

1. Godly relationships have one primary leader, e.g. God, Jesus Christ, the human husband, the parents, or the master (supervisor at work).

2. Godly leaders must lead with godly leadership.

3. Godly leaders have a responsibility to act in godly ways, and to ensure godly activity from those under their authority.

4. When the leader is godly but the subordinate is not, the leader will give longsuffering love for the purpose of restoration.

5. When longsuffering love does bring reform, then godly discipline is needed.

6. Godly discipline includes "putting away," or some equivalent separation for a temporary period.

7. If the leader continues to be godly, but the subordinate continues with ungodly activities, then divorce may become "required." A special NOTE is made about this situation:

In the Ephesians passage quoted earlier, Christ is seen giving Himself up for the Church. A blame-shifting wife may use this principle to take ungodly advantage of her husband. He should keep the rest of that context in mind. He might even remind his wife that the *true* bride of Christ is obliged to do two things. *First,* she allows herself to be washed (and cleansed) by the Word of God so that she becomes blameless—without blemish or stain. This means that the husband must "constantly" be into the Word of God, with a heart full of love for God and his wife. *Second,* she actively participates by making herself "ready," for her husband (Revelation 19:7). And we should of course mention that husbands also can become ungodly blame-shifters....

--But what if the leader is not godly and wants rid of his subordinate (wife)...

8. If the leader is not godly and the subordinate is godly, then the "leader" likely has only one choice, and that is divorce. Jesus said that Moses commanded, or permitted, divorce due to their hardness of heart. He was probably referring to the husbands (although in some cases it would have been the wife, or even both spouses). Such divorce required a certificate so that the "innocent" ex-wife could remarry if she chose to do so.

9. If this same ungodly leader is vengeful, he may "put away" his wife without a certificate of divorce. He may also take another wife, or concubine. His first wife may not marry without being "guilty" of legalistic adultery. This hateful act may be found in Malachi 2:16, as translated by the King James Version. The "put away" wife may have the faith to wait any number of years to find a gloriously renewed marriage. On the other hand, she may need to make other plans. Please note that this situation and the one above, when considered together, do again call to mind the tremendous difference between divorce and "put away."

--And what if the leader (husband) is lukewarm but the subordinate (wife) is a Spirit filled Christian...?

10. This opens up a whole new ball game. For example she may want to live a simple lifestyle in order to give extra money to the church, and world missions. He may want new and expensive housing, and vehicles—even an indoor swimming pool. They will both need to balance their desires and burdens with the risks & gains for all concerned—and proceed in some godly manner—even if it is not ideal. Prayer should help....

The list of what-if's could go on and on; but this is an epilogue, so we should stop. I hope that the "long view" has made its own point well enough by now. I hope that the reader has seen the pattern with sufficient clarity to come to his or her own godly conclusion for most any situation. If not, then gather together any number of godly folks and a godly answer should surely come forth.

This epilogue has been a bit long. However, its theme is in a league of its own, and it seemed to deserve more status than being just another chapter. As this epilogue is ended, a few more thoughts are given, for whatever they may be worth. One is an attempt to show that I am aware of the dangers of male chauvinism. In any number of places in this book, I have allowed the interchange of male and female. This cannot always be done but wherever practicable, the reader is welcomed and encouraged to do so. Moreover, if Adam had been the first to sin—instead of Eve, then 1st Corinthians 11:1-3 might just have had the following "pecking" order: God, Jesus Christ, the woman, and then the man—instead of God, Jesus Christ, the man, and then the woman. Please also keep in mind two related issues. *First,* more is often caught, than taught. *Second,* we humans have inborn rebellion and need an almost constant example of submission. Children reared in a home with a godly "pecking" order have a huge head start on life. Those who are not given this ingrained trait will likely have trouble with authority—for as long as they live.

This book has had its starts and stops. Therefore, its style is not entirely uniform. Hopefully, this makes it a bit more interesting. This book was not part of a Doctor of Divinity degree—although one might wish that it were. It is therefore without that polish that comes from the halls of ivy. But with that polish, I might not have been bold enough to make some of the more contentious points—that I believe the good Lord wanted me to make.

It has been thrilling for me to "see" several special helps from the good Lord in finishing this book. However, I am still somewhat tentative about all its conclusions. I am willing to admit that some conclusions may be flawed. On the other hand, my burden for these conclusions to become available to the family of believers is now lifted—and that has been worth the risks taken.

As you may notice this book is self-published. It was, however, not written from inside a fishbowl. A good amount of outside influence has not only been allowed but also welcomed, in a variety of ways. At least one nationally known and respected author read it and gave critique. Several other experts have given small but weighty input, especially in the area of Jewish culture.

In my innumerable meditations about *Divorce as "Required" by Scripture,* I believe that I have felt the forceful hand of the Holy Spirit upon me many times. A verse that has come to me rather often in the writing of this book is Matthew 11:12, along with 11:11 and some underlining:

"I tell you the truth: Among those born of women there has not risen anyone greater than John the Baptist; yet he who is least in the kingdom of heaven is greater than he. 12 From the days of John the Baptist until now, the kingdom of heaven has been forcefully advancing, and forceful men lay hold of it. NIV

Changing the direction of a large pendulum, like Jewish tradition or church tradition about divorce and remarriage, takes a lot of force. One would not want the pendulum to swing too far—once its gets redirected. Therefore, I have tried to apply godly forces with moderation, objectivity and integrity. To whatever degree I have failed, may God be gracious to me. To whatever extent this book may give godly help to victims of ungodly marriages, may the Father in Heaven be given the honor and the glory, in Jesus' name, Amen.

Bibliography, by Category

BIBLES quoted

International Bible Society. The Holy Bible, New International Version. Grand Rapids, MI: The Zondervan Corporation, 1973, 1978, 1984.

Wuest, Kenneth S. The New Testament: An Expanded Version. Grand Rapids, MI: William B. Eerdmans Publishing Company, Reprinted 2002.

Zondervan Publishing House. Authorized King James Version. Grand Rapids, MI: Zondervan Publishing House.

BIBLES reviewed (well-known and therefore listed without bibliography data)

American Standard Version (1901)
Amplified New Testament
Contemporary English Version
God's Word (1995)
Good News Version
J.B. Phillips (New Testament)
Jerusalem Bible
King James Version
Living Bible
Moffatt's Bible Translation
New American Bible
New King James Version
New English Bible
New Revised Standard
Revised English Bible
Revised Standard

BOOKS

Adams, Jay E. Marriage, Divorce & Remarriage, in the Bible. Grand Rapids, MI: Zondervan Publishing House, 1980.

Coblentz, John. What the Bible Says About Divorce & Remarriage. Harrisonburg, VA: Christian Light Publications, Inc., 1992.

Cosby, Michael R. Sex in the Bible, An Introduction to What Scriptures Teach Us About Sexuality. Englewood Cliffs NJ: Prentice-Hall, Inc., 1984.

Crouzel, Henri. L'Eglise Primitive Face au Divorce. Paris: Editions Beauchesne, 1971.

Crouzel, Henri; Translated by A.S. Worrall. Origen. San Francisco, CA: Harper & Row, Publishers, 1989.

Duty, Guy. Divorce & Remarriage. Minneapolis, MN: Bethany House Publishers, 1967, 1983.

Gothard, Bill. Rebuilders Guide, Supplement. Oak Brook, IL: Institute in Basic Life Principles, 1983.

Heth, William A, and Gordon J. Wenham. Jesus and Divorce. Nashville, TN: Thomas Nelson, Inc., 1984.

House, H. Wayne, ed. Contributions from J. Carl Laney, William Heth, Thomas Edgar, and Larry Richards. Divorce and Remarriage, Four Christian Views. Downers Grove, IL: Intervarsity Press, 1990.

Metzger, Bruce M, and Michael D. Coogan, eds. The Oxford Companion to the Bible. New York, NY: Oxford University Press, 1993.

Metzger, Bruce Manning. The New Testament, its background, growth, and content. Nashville, TN: Abingdon Press, 1965.

Porter, Jack Nusan, ed. Women in Chains, A Sourcebook on the Agunah. Northvale, NJ: Jason Aaronson Inc, 1995.

Richards, Larry. Remarrriage: A Healing Gift from God. Waco, TX: Word Incorporated, 1981.

Van Impe, Dr. Jack. Alcohol: The Beloved Enemy. Troy, MI: Jack Van Impe Ministries, 1980.

Whiston, William, A.M. translator. Josephus, Complete Works. Grand Rapids, MI: Kregel Publications, 1978.

White, James R. The King James Only Controversy. Minneapolis, MN: Bethany House Purlishers, 1995.

Willmington, Harold L; Willmington's Guide to the Bible. Wheaton, IL: Victor Books, 1987.

COMMENTARIES

Cole, R.Alan, Ph.D. Exodus, An Introduction and Commentary. Downers Grove, IL: Inter-Varsity Press, 1973.

Cranfield, C.E.B. The Gospel According to Saint Mark. Cambridge, ENG: Cambridge University Press, 1966.

Davidson, Professor F., M.A., D.D. The New Bible Commentary. Grand Rapids, MI: Wm B. Eerdmans Publishing Company, Reprinted 1963.

Dowd, Sharyn E. Reading Mark. Macon, GA: Smyth & Helwys Publishing, Inc., 2000.

Edwards, James R. The Gospel According to Mark. Grand Rapids, MI: Wm. B. Eerdmans Publishing Co., 2002.

Feinberg, Charles L. The Minor Prophets. Chicago, IL: Moody Press, Combined Edition, 1976.

Gispen, W.H; Translated by Ed van der Maas. Exodus. Grand Rapids, MI: Zondervan Publishing House, 1982.

Gundry, Robert H. Mark, A Commentary On His Apology for the Cross. Grand Rapids, MI: Wm. B. Eerdmans Publishing Co., 1993.

Hare, Douglas R.A. Mark (Westminster Bible Companion). Louisville, KY: Westminster John Know Press, 1996.

Hiebert, D. Edmond. Mark, A Portrait of A Servant. Chicago, IL: Moody Press, 1974.

Ironside, H.A., Litt.D. Expository Notes on the Gospel of Matthew. Neptune, NJ: Loizeaux Brothers, 1948.

Ironside, H.A. Litt.D. Expository Notes on the Gospel of Mark. Neptune, NJ: Loizeaux Brothers, 1948.

Keener, Craig S. The IVP Bible Background Commentary, New Testament. Downers Grove, IL: InterVarsity Press, 1993.

LaVerdiere, Eugene. The Beginning of the Gospel: Introducing the Gospel According to Mark. Collegeville, MN: The Order of St. Benedict, Inc., 1999.

Mackintosh, C.H. Notes on the Pentateuch, Genesis to Deuteronomy. Neptune, NJ: Loizeaux Brothers, 1972.

Mason, Rex. The Books of Haggai, Zechariah and Malachi. Cambridge, ENG: Cambridge University Press, 1972.

McComiskey, Thomas Edward, II. The Minor Prophets (Hosea through Malachi). Grand Rapids, MI: Baker Book House Company, 1998.

McKenna, David L; with Lloyd J. Ogilvie, gen. ed. The Communicators Commentary—Mark. Dallas, TX: Word Publishing, 1982.

Oden, Thomas C., and Christopher A. Hall, eds. Mark. Downers Grove, IL: InterVarsity Press, 1998

Richards, Lawrence O. The Teachers Commentary. Wheaton, IL: Victor Books, 1987.

Walvoord, John F. and Roy B. Zuck, eds. The Bible Knowledge Commentary. Wheaton, IL: Victor Books, 1985.

Wessel, Walter W. The Expositor's Bible Commentary, with The New International Version—Mark. Grand Rapids, MI: Zondervan Publishing House, 1995.

Willoughby, W. Robert. First Corinthians. Camp Hill, PA: Christian Publications, Inc.

COMMENTARIES, Parallel.

The Bethany Parallel Commentary on the Old Testament. Minneapolis, MN: Bethany House Publishers, 1985.
---Matthew Henry's Commentary on the Whole Bible, 1960,
---Adam Clarke's Commentary on the Whole Bible, 1967,
---The Jamieson, Fausset, and Brown Commenary.

The Bethany Parallel Commenary on the New Testament.
Same as above---Henry, Clarke, J., F., & B.

DICTIONARIES

Johnson, Samuel. A Dictionary of the English Language, (1755). London, ENG: Times Books, 1979.

Little, William; with H.W. Fowler and Jessie Coulson. The Shorter Oxford English Dictionary. London, ENG: Oxford University Press, 1973.

Webster, Noah. Webster's New Twentieth Century Dictionary of the English Language, Unabridged, second edition. Cleveland, OH: World Publishing Company, 1974.

ENCYCLOPEDIAS, HARMONY, HANDBOOK(s), SAYINGS, WORDBOOKS, ETC.

Archer, Gleason L. Encyclopedia of Bible Difficulties. Grand Rapids, MI: Regency Reference Library, Zondervan Publishing House, 1982.

Bercot, David W., ed. A Dictionary of Early Christian Beliefs. Peabody, MA: Hendrickson Publishers, Inc., 1998.

Bratcher, Robert G, and Eugene A. Nida. A Translator's Handbook on the Gospel of Mark. London, New York: United Bible Societies, 1961.

Clark, David J, and Howard A. Hatton. A Handbook on Haggai, Zechariah, and Malachi. New York, NY: United Bible Societies, 2002.

Harris, R. Laird, ed; Gleason L Archer, Jr, and Bruce K. Watke, Associate Eds. Theological Wordbook of the Old Testament. Chicago, IL: Moody Bible Institute, 1980.

Kaiser, Walter C., Jr; Peter H. Davids, F.F. Bruce, and Manfred T. Brauch. Hard Sayings of the Bible. Downers Grove, IL: InterVarsity Press,1996.

Newman, Barclay M; Philip Stine. A Translator's Handbook on the Gospel of Matthew. London, New York: United Bible Societies, 1988.

Packer, James I; Merrill C. Tenney, A.M., Ph.D. and William White Jr., Th.M., Ph.D. The Bible Almanac. Nashville, TN: Thomas Nelson Publishers, 1980.

Pentecost, J. Dwight. Edited by Doris Rikkers. A Harmony of the Words and Works of Jesus Christ, (from the New International Version). Grand Rapids, MI: Academie Books, The Zondervan Corporation, 1981.

Reiling, J., and J.L. Swellengrebel. A Translator's Handbook on the Gospel of Luke. London, New York: United Bible Societies, 1971.

Tenney, Merril C., gen. ed; and Steven Barabas, associate. The Zondervan Pictorial Encyclopedia of the Bible, (five volumes). Grand Rapids, MI: Regency Reference Library, Zondervan Publishing House, 1982.

Wight, Fred H. Manners and Customs of Bible Lands. Chicago, IL: Moody Press, 1953.

Wilmington, Harold L. Survey of the Old Testament. Wheaton, IL: Victor Books, 1987.

EXEGETICAL, EXPOSITORY & THEOLOGICAL DICTIONARIES

Balz, Horst, and Gerhard Schneider. Exegetical Dictionary of the New Testament. Grand Rapids, MI: William B. Eerdmans Publishing Company, 1990.

Brown, Colin; gen. ed. The New International Dictionary of New Testament Theology. Grand Rapids, MI: Zondervan Publishing House, 1975-1978.

Davis, John D., Ph.D., D.D. A Dictionary of the Bible. Philadelphia, PA: Westminster Press, 1898.

Earle, Ralph, Th.D. Word Meanings in the New Testament. Grand Rapids, MI: Baker Book House, 2nd print, 1987.

Richards, Lawrence O. Expository Dictionary of Bible Words. Grand Rapids, MI: Zondervan Publishing House, 1985.

Unger, Merrill F. The New Unger's Bible Dictionary. Chicago, IL: Moody Press, 1988.

VanGemeren, William A. New International Dictionary of Old Testament Theology and Exegesis. Grand Rapids, MI: Zondervan Publishing House, 1977.

Vine, W.E. Vine's Amplified Expository Dictionary of New Testament Words. Iowa Falls, IO: World Bible Publishers, Inc., 1991.

GREEK & HEBREW TOOLS

Arndt, William F, and F. Wilbur Gingrich. A Greek-English Lexicon of the New Testament. Chicago, IL: The University of Chicago Press, 1958.

Gesenius, H.W.F. Gesenius Hebrew-Chaldee Lexicon to the Old Testament. Grand Rapids, MI: Baker Book House, 1979.

Davidson, Benjamin. The Analytical Hebrew and Chaldee Lexicon. Grand Rapids, MI: Zondervan Publishing House, 1980.

Green, Jay P. Sr. The Interlinear Bible. Lafayette, IN: Sovereign Grace Publishers, 1986.

Goodrick, Edward W., and John R. Kohlenberg III. The NIV Exhaustive Concordance. Grand Rapids, MI: Zondervan Publishing House, 1990.

Kohlenberger, John R., III, ed. The NIV Interlinear Hebrew-English Old Testament. Grand Rapids, MI: Regency Reference Library, an imprint of Zondervan Publishing House, 1987.

Marshall, Alfred. The NIV Interlinear Greek-English New Testament. Grand Rapids, MI: Zondervan Publishing House, 1976.

Strong, James, LL.D., S.T.D. The New Strong's Complete Dictionary of Bible Words. Nashville, TN: Thomas Nelson Publishers, 1996.

Strong, James, LL.D., S.T.D. The New Strong's Exhaustive Concordance of the Bible. Nashville, TN: Thomas Nelson Publishers, 1984.

Thayer, Joseph Henry, D.D. A Greek-English Lexicon of the New Testament. Grand Rapids, MI: Zondervan Publishing House, 1982.

Vanderpool, Charles; and Terry Neimann. The Apostolic Bible. Newport, OR: The Apostolic Press, 2003.

Wigram, George V. The Analytical Greek Lexicon of the New Testament. Peabody, MA: Hendrickson Publishers, 1983.

Young, Robert, LL.D. Analytical Concordance to the Bible. Grand Rapids, MI: Wm B. Eerdmans Publishing, 1970.

JEWISH INFORMATION

Amram, David Werner. Jewish Encyclopedia.com. "Agunah" article, 2002.

Barsky, Rabbi Dr. David L. Judaism and the Church: Past, Present and Future. Pompono Beach, FL: Beth Hillel Press, 1999.

Blackman, Philip, F.C.S. Tractate Gittin. New York, NY: The Judaica Press Inc., 1963.

Dorff, (Rabbi) Elliot, and Arthur Rosett. A Living Tree. Albany, NY: State University of New York Press, 1988.

Neusner, Jacob. The Mishnah, A New Translation. New Haven, CN: Yale University Press, 1988.

Porter, Jack Nusan, ed. Women in Chains, A Sourcebook on the Agunah. Northvale, NJ: Jason Aaronson Inc, 1995.

Wegner, Judith Romney. Chattel or Person? New York, NY: Oxford University Press, 1988.

JOURNALS, MAGAZINES, ETC.

Bird, Warren. "Stanley Dilemma Underscores Troubled Clergy Marriages." Christianity Today October 23, 1995: 82-83.

Board of Bishops. "Marriage." This We Confess, A Statement of Christian Faith, for the Brethren in Christ Church Second Edition, June 1971: 12.

Callison, Walter L. "Divorce, the Law, and Jesus." Your Church May/June 1986: 18-23.

Heth, William A. "Jesus on Divorce: How My Mind Has Changed." The Southern Baptist Journal of Theology Volume 6, Number 1 (Spring 2002): 4-29.

Poll, Rich. "Exegeting Bill Gothard." Christianity Today March 2003: 77-78.

Ross, R. A. "Divorces 'Required' by Scripture." Shalom! Volume 16, Number 2 (Spring 1996): 8-9.

Wenham, Gordon. "Does the New Testament Approve Remarriage after Divorce?" The Southern Baptist Journal of Theology Volume 6, Number 1 (Spring 2002): 30-45.

SEPTUAGINT

Brenton, Sir Lancelot C.L. The Septuagint with Apocrypha: Greek and English. Grand Rapids, MI: Zondervan Publishing House, 7th printing—1980; originally published in London, 1851.

Hatch, Edwin, M.A., D.D, and Henry A. Redpath, M.A. A Concordance to the Septuagint. Grand Rapids, MI: Baker Book House, 1983.

Vanderpool, Charles; and Terry Neimann. The Apostolic Bible. Newport, OR: The Apostolic Press, 2003.

SOFTWARE

BIBLESOFT, Inc. PC Study Bible, Advanced Reference Library. Seattle, WA: Biblesoft, Inc. 1988-2005.

Sources not listed elsewhere include:
---Barnes' Notes on the Old & New Testament (Commentary)
---Fausset's Bible Dictionary
---International Standard Bible Encyclopedia
---Keil & Delitzsch Old Testament Commentary
---Nelson's Bible Dictionary

---Robertson's New Testament Word Pictures
---Vincent's Word Studies in the New Testament
---Wycliffe Bible Commentary

WEBSITES

deeperdoctrine.com for additional information about this book; and for ministry information on other subjects, e.g. a seminar on "Anguish Annuls Anger."

gospelminutes.org for the article "Divorced or Put Away?" a listing of original languages' word use in Old and New Testaments.

http://home.earthlink.net/~truth/sec8-4-2Marriage.html for the original article by Walter L. Callison "Divorce, the Law, and Jesus."

Index of Scriptures

Note: Parentheses have been used in this Index to indicate a range of verses that are not specifically identified in the actual text of the book. For example, the Parable of the Sower is listed above as (13:1-23), of Matthew. Page 132 lists that parable—but without a specific textual reference.

NOTES

NOTES

NOTES

Divorce as 'Required' by Scripture Order Form

Use this convenient form to order the book:
Divorce as 'Required' by Scripture

Please Print:

Name____

Address______________________________________

City____

State______________________ **Zip**______________

Phone (   ) ________________________________

______ copies of book @ $12.95 each $___________

Postage & Handling @ $4.00 each $___________

TOTAL amount enclosed $ ___________

Please make checks payable to: **Deeper Doctrine**

And send to: **P.O. Box 291**
Grantham, PA
17027-0291

ORDER

BLANK

ON

REVERSE

SIDE